Risk Assessment Handbook

by Ron Akass TD, MIOSH, RSP

Legal Editor
Mark Tyler at CMS Cameron McKenna

Tolley

ISBN 0 75450 224–4

Published by
Tolley
2 Addiscombe Road
Croydon
Surrey
CR9 5AF
0181–662 2000

℞ A member of the Reed Elsevier plc group

© Tolley

Typeset in Great Britain by
York House Typographic Ltd, London

Printed and bound in Great Britain by
Redwood Books Limited, Trowbridge, Wiltshire

Table of Contents

Chapter 4   Risk Assessment — Preparation

Chapter 5   Risk Assessment — Methodology

Table of Cases

Table of Statutes

Table of Statutory Instruments

List of Tables

1 Introduction

Aim

1.1 The aim of this handbook is twofold: first to provide an explanation of the background to risk assessment, describing the requirements of the law in this regard and how to develop risk assessments while ensuring that they remain relevant. The second and subordinate aim is to remove the 'mystique' which has grown around the subject of risk assessment in recent years.

Roles and responsibilities

1.2 Everyone at work has some responsibility in relation to risk assessment, none more so than managers, irrespective of their role or seniority. Indeed, every person who has a degree of responsibility for the work of others has by definition a key role in the risk assessment process.

It is frequently emphasised that workplace health and safety is a matter for everyone at work, and this contention could not be more apposite than in respect to risk assessment. The notion that managers can unilaterally decide what risks their subordinates are exposed to without taking account of the views of those actually doing the work, is not only bad management but, *prima facie*, a breach of the legislation concerned with employee consultation on health and safety matters.

A number of people have jobs or job responsibilities which require them to have a good understanding of the aims and objectives of the legislation concerned with risk assessment, and accepted 'best practice' in complying with it. Examples are competent health and safety advisers appointed to assist the employer in discharging his various health and safety duties under the law; Trade Union and elected health and safety representatives; human resources (personnel) staff; lawyers; and second level managers and above, who will have to review the risk assessments of their subordinate managers.

Finally there are those who actually carry out the work of the firm or organisation, and are therefore 'at the sharp end'. Nobody has a greater or more relevant contribution to make to the risk assessment process.

1.3   Introduction

While subsequent chapters develop and discuss roles and responsibilities in respect to risk assessment in detail, it will be clear from the above that this handbook provides a work tool for everyone at work, irrespective of their job or status in the business or organisation.

Evolution of risk assessment

1.3   The *Health and Safety at Work Act etc. 1974* (*HSWA*) is, and is likely to remain, the principal health and safety statute in the United Kingdom. The numerous health and safety regulations introduced since 1974, including those ratifying European Union (EU) directives, were all brought into force under the aegis of HSWA.

Health neglected

1.4   Notwithstanding the huge advances in health and safety brought about by *HSWA*, there was, until 1988, an absence of specific regulations addressing the risks to health arising from substances used at work, or from workplace conditions and operations that produced dusts and fumes. The *Control of Substances Hazardous to Health Regulations 1988* (*COSHH*) were introduced under the aegis of *HSWA* in order to address this omission.

The Control of Substances Hazardous to Health Regulations 1988

1.5   These are frequently amended, most recently in 1999. When the *COSHH* regulations first appeared, they were widely considered to be the most important and far-reaching of any health and safety measure introduced since the passing of *HSWA* in 1974, since they filled the gap in legislation covering the 'health' element of the health and safety equation.

'Self-assessment' first mentioned

1.6   In addition to its impact in terms of the health of workers, *COSHH* was also the first regulation in the health and safety field calling for the development of 'assessments' by employers with the objective in this case of ensuring that the substances they used, workplace conditions they experienced and processes which they performed did not pose a risk to the health of their employees.

Slow compliance with COSHH

1.7 Full compliance with the requirements of *COSHH*, in particular in respect to assessments, has been a slow process, and there is evidence that there are still some organisations who have not fully complied with these important regulations, although they were first enacted over ten years ago.

Cultural change

1.8 The explanation for this is undoubtedly the cultural change heralded by the *COSHH* regulations which called for management action to address health hazards to be preceded by an assessment process aimed at identification and quantification of the risks as a precursor to action.

Employers are required by the *COSHH* regulations to carry out an assessment to determine whether they use hazardous substances, have suitable workplace conditions, or follow work processes which produced potentially hazardous dust/fumes, and to take measures to eliminate the danger or reduce the risks posed to an acceptable level.

It is perhaps not surprising that such a dramatic change in the method of compliance called for in the *COSHH* regulations, compared to the customary approach of spelling out precisely what employers need to do, or what specific standards of performance were required, would result in uncertainty and delay in conforming.

A full description of the requirements of the COSHH regulations appears in Chapter 8 *Statutory Requirements – Part 3.*

Effect of European Union Directives

1.9 During the course of 1992, in response to EEC directives on health and safety, and in anticipation of the formal inception of the European Single Market on 1 January 1993, six new health and safety related regulations were enacted in the UK, to take effect on 1 January 1993. Three of these regulations allowed periods of transition before full compliance was required.

Of these six new regulations, colloquially referred to as 'the six pack', by far the most important from a risk assessment standpoint, is the *Management of Health and Safety at Work Regulations 1992 (MHSWR)*, which, in *regulation 3*, calls for employers to develop risk assessments in respect of *all of their operations*, not just those in which substances were used or dust/fume producing conditions pertained.

Risk assessment for all work activities required

1.10   Thus in January 1993, Great Britain, which had given birth to the Industrial Revolution some 200 years before, enacted regulations for the first time calling for employers to develop risk assessments addressing the risks to which their employees and others not in their employment might be exposed as a consequence of the employers operations.

Throughout the whole of the previous 200 years workers had been fatally, seriously or slightly injured as a consequence of their work, and huge numbers had their lives cut short by work related ill-health, yet it took until 1993 to require employers to consider in a formal way why these things happened and what they must do to stop them happening, not only to their own employees, but to anybody else who comes onto the firms premises or who can be adversely affected by the way it operates.

Risk assessment as good practice

1.11   The requirement to develop risk assessments was not an onerous task for those for whom such assessments were part of their normal or routine management of the business. How indeed could they comply with the key requirement to produce and keep updated their health and safety policy – a novel yet key requirement of *HSWA*, if they did not consider the health and safety risks created by or incidental to their business operations?

Risk assessment pivotal to EU approach to health and safety

1.12   While the risk assessment requirement in *regulation 3* of *MHSWR* is paramount, and is probably the most onerous and important of all the measures called for in the six health and safety regulations introduced on 1 January 1993, it is not the only regulation which calls for assessment.

Indeed the other five regulations each call for assessment, either directly or by implication. For example the *Health and Safety (Display Screen Equipment) Regulations* (*DSE*) and the *Manual Handling Operations Regulations* (*MHO*) specifically call for assessments, while the *Personal Protective Equipment Regulations* (*PPE*) leave no doubt about the need to assess what PPE should be specified for particular activities, while the *Health, Safety and Welfare* (*HSW*) and *Provision and Use of Work Equipment Regulations* (*PUWER*) (since re-issued) each impose requirements, which, if not satisfied, suggest that the exposure thus created should be addressed by the 'general' risk assessment within *regulation 3* of *MHSWR*.

Scope of coverage of risk assessment requirements in this handbook

1.13 In addition to providing detailed information and guidance on compliance with the requirement for risk assessment contained in *regulation 3* of *MHSWR* – often referred to as the 'general' risk assessment, this handbook also discusses assessments called for directly or indirectly in other regulations, some of which have been referred to in passing in this chapter.

Wider change brought about by the risk assessment requirement

1.14 The requirement for employers to assess the risks in their business has stimulated re-examination of the role and nomenclature of those involved directly with workplace health and safety, and whose job titles, depending upon their seniority/experience/qualifications, has traditionally been Safety Manager or Health and Safety Manager/adviser or officer. Were these key people managing health and safety, or managing risks to prevent them having an impact upon health and safety? Are risks in the workplace confined solely to those affecting people? Patently not.

There will be risks to the product, risks to the environment, risks to the image of the company, and of course general commercial risks. While the requirement for risk assessment contained in *MHSWR* relates to the health and safety of people, it is clear that there are a great many risks in the workplace which, although not necessarily endangering people, could certainly endanger the prosperity – even the survival – of a business.

The common thread in all these undesirable and unwanted events is 'risk', and if risks are to be prevented altogether – or if this is not possible – their severity or consequences reduced, they have to be managed. Therefore the science is that of 'Risk Management' not 'Health and Safety Management'.

As more firms are appreciating this fact, they are adopting different job titles; health and safety managers are becoming 'risk managers' or advisers, and consulting firms in this field are changing their titles to 'risk management consultants'. It can only be a matter of time before the traditional title 'safety manager' or the like disappears altogether.

In paragraph 1.1 it was stated that the secondary aim of this handbook is to remove the mystique that has grown around the subject of risk assessment. Hopefully this explanation of the background to job title changes has gone some way toward that. Today's 'risk manager' was yesterday's 'safety manager'.

Practical limitations

1.15   In paragraph 1.14 the scope of risk in business was considered, together with the changes in job titles and descriptions to reflect current thinking on this subject.

It is important to stress that while a risk manager's role could reasonably encompass risks to people, product and the environment, or a combination of these, it could not and should not include general commercial risks, and these will only be referred to in this handbook where other risks could potentially affect the continuing commercial viability of the enterprise.

2 Statutory Requirements for Risk Assessment — Part 1

Principal legislation concerned with risk assessment

2.1 This chapter discusses the principal regulations dealing with risk assessment – the *Management of Health and Safety at Work Regulations 1992 (MHSWR)*.

Although *regulation 3* of *MHSWR* deals specifically with risk assessment, most regulations concerned with health and safety that have come into force since 1992 also make reference to risk assessment. These regulations fall into one of two classifications:

(i) Where the regulations emphasise the importance of taking account of any risks germane to the subject matter of the regulations, as part of the development of the 'general' risk assessment undertaken to comply with *MHSWR*. For example, the *Provision and Use of Work Equipment Regulations 1998 (PUWER)*. (See Chapter 8.)

(ii) Regulations dealing with discrete work activities which of necessity require risk assessments relating to them to be more focused, although following the general principles for risk assessment in *MHSWR*. These regulations contain more detailed guidance on the risk assessment to be carried out to comply with them as well as requiring special documentation relating to the assessment. Examples are the *Health and Safety (Display Screen Equipment) Regulations 1992 (DSE)* and the *Manual Handling Operations Regulations 1992 (MHO)*. (See Chapter 3.)

Risk assessment requirements of the *Management of Health and Safety at Work Regulations 1992 (MHSWR)*

2.2 Although *regulation 3* of *MHSWR* is concerned solely with risk assessment, most of the other constituent regulations within *MHSWR* include requirements which have relevance to the risk assessment process, either directly or indirectly, and these requirements must be taken into account when developing or reviewing existing risk assessments. Table 1 summarises these regulations.

2.2   Statutory Requirements for Risk Assessment

Table 1 – Regulations within *MHSWR* (as amended) which have relevance to risk assessment

Regulation number and title	Requirement
Reg 3 Risk assessment	Every employer and self-employed person must develop risk assessments, taking account of risks to employees and others who could be affected by their operations. They must publish 'significant findings' if the work-force exceeds four. Assessments must be kept under review. This is *the* key regulation relating to risk assessment.
Reg 4 Health & safety arrangements	Employers must make arrangements for the planning, organisation, control, monitoring and review of the measures taken to control risks – see paragraph 2.6.
Reg 5 Health surveillance	Employers to provide health surveillance for employees if a need is identified by the risk assessment – see paragraph 2.7.
Reg 6 Health and Safety advisers	Employers to appoint one or more competent health and safety advisers to assist them in complying with H&S law/regulations – see paragraph 2.8.
Reg 7 Procedures for serious and imminent danger	Employers to have procedures to address serious and imminent danger and to nominate staff to manage implementation – see paragraph 2.9.
	Fire will feature large in these procedures as *regulation 3* (Risk assessment) has been amended to specifically require fire risk to be addressed within the general risk assessment – see Chapter 8.
Reg 8 Information for employees	All employees must be told about the risk assessment findings and the measures taken to eliminate or mitigate the risks identified – see paragraph 2.10.
Reg 9 Co-operation and co-ordination	Where employers and/or self-employed persons share a workplace, each must provide the others with details of their risk assessment, where the assessment includes risks which could affect those sharing the workplace with them – see paragraph 2.11.

Reg 10	Persons working in host employers' or self-employed persons' undertakings	Duty upon host employers to inform the employer of employees who are to work in his premises about any risks to which those employees might be exposed and the measures taken to manage the risks, and to convey the same information to the employees themselves before they commence work in his premises – see paragraph 2.12.
Reg 11	Capabilities and training	Requires employers to provide additional health and safety training where changes in the working environment, work processes, etc. alter the risk profile – see paragraph 2.13.
Reg 12	Employees duties	Employees are required to report to their employer or a nominated person details of any serious or imminent danger or other shortcoming in the health and safety arrangements which has the propensity to affect them. Such reports would indicate that risks existed which had not been envisaged by the company risk assessment – see paragraph 2.14.
Reg 13	Temporary workers	Insofar as risks are concerned, a temporary worker should receive the same information about emergency procedures and risks to his health and safety as a person working in a host employers premises – see *regulation 10* above.
Reg 13A *Reg 13B* *Reg 13C*	New or expectant mothers	Requires employers to assess the work normally undertaken by pregnant employees to identify any risks which the work poses to them or to the unborn child, and to initiate measures to protect them where appropriate – see Chapter 7.
Reg 13D	Children and young persons	Special risk assessments must be undertaken before young persons commence work, taking account of their relative immaturity and other factors. Where the person is below the school leaving age, their parent or guardian must receive details of the special risk assessment before they commence work – see Chapter 7.

Risk assessment – the common thread

2.3   Many of the requirements in respect to risk assessment referred to in Table 1 above are discussed in this or other chapters, with the objective of emphasising that virtually all of the constituent regulations of *MHSWR* have a common thread or message – that of managing risks.

2.4 Statutory Requirements for Risk Assessment

Risk assessment is not simply a matter of deciding what risks exist in a workplace, assessing them, taking measures to eliminate or ameliorate them and keeping records. Other factors have a bearing on the assessment; it must be undertaken within the context of legislation covering a wide spectrum of human activity, in respect to some workers who fall into special categories, and in some cases and for some risks, developed in co-operation with others with whom an employer may share the workplace.

Where the activities of contractors are concerned, recent judgments show that employers can be held culpable in situations where their contractors either had accidents or were the prime cause of accidents, and this has served to emphasise how exposed an employer (client) can be when commissioning contractors to do work which they are technically not competent to do themselves. Chapter 9 discusses these cases.

Risk assessment – *regulation 3 MHSWR*

2.4 The key requirements of *regulation 3* are:

— employers must carry out 'suitable and sufficient' risk assessments taking account of risks to their employees and others not in their employment which are posed by the way the business is operated;

— the duty to consider others is also imposed upon the self-employed, who must also carry out a 'personal' risk assessment;

— to consider and implement measures to remove the risks identified altogether or reduce them to an acceptable level;

— to review risk assessments whenever there are changes to the 'status quo' which affect the existing risk profile;

— where there are five or more employees, the 'significant findings' of the assessment must be recorded and this record must identify any group of employees who are considered to be especially at risk.

No reference is made in *regulation 3* to communicating details of the risk assessment to employees, as this important requirement appears in *regulation 8* – information for employees – see paragraph 2.11.

'Suitable and sufficient'

2.5   This key qualifying statement about the standard to be attained when developing risk assessments appears in the first line of *regulation 3*. This definition will clearly be an important consideration in the event that a risk assessment is deemed to be below the standard expected.

Guidance is that to be suitable and sufficient, the assessment should:

(a)   identify the significant risks associated with the work;

(b)   enable those developing the assessment to determine what needs to be done to comply with any statutory requirements applicable to the work or process;

(c)   be appropriate to the risk and able to offer protection for a reasonable period of time.

The above guidance is expanded in the ACOP, but in the final analysis a risk assessment, irrespective of the method used when developing it, will be subjective. This is not to say that subjectivity is wrong.

If a risk assessment is undertaken by those who actually do the work – or are close to the operation, they should know more about the subject and about the risks associated with it than anyone else.

Notes on the regulation 3 requirement

(i) Risk assessments called for in other regulations

2.6   Paragraph 2.1(ii) has referred to regulations which call for a discrete risk assessment solely related to the subject of the regulations in question. In order to comply with the (general) risk assessment in *MHSWR*, it is not necessary to repeat the assessment made to comply with these regulations or to incorporate the findings with those of the (general) assessment.

For completeness sake the general assessment might include reference to these other assessments, and it is recommended that the 'master' copies of all the assessments be kept together.

(ii) Standards

When considering the measures necessary to remove or mitigate risks, it is important to take account of standards already established in regulations, approved codes of practice (ACOPs), HSE guidance, trade or professional publications, manufacturers. or suppliers manuals or recommendations and other relevant guidance.

Statutory requirements must be complied with. If Approved Codes of Practice are not followed, this might be cited in the event of prosecution as evidence, and the onus will be upon the offending organisation to prove that their arrangements/method of working are as good as those described in the ACOP.

(iii) Hazards not included in the risk assessment

In all workplaces hazards will appear regularly, usually as the result of general wear and tear upon the building fabric, fittings and equipment. These problems are often referred to as 'maintenance matters' and all businesses should have procedures to deal with them.

Where there is an 'in-house' maintenance unit, problems may be reported to the unit by telephone, or a maintenance form completed. In smaller organisations a contract is often entered into calling for the nominated contractor to attend to deal with problems within a stipulated time, or at once if the problem is serious. Where these arrangements exist, it is useful to have an appointed 'in-house' co-ordinator to interface with the nominated contractor.

Whatever the arrangements, maintenance problems are usually attended to within days rather than weeks. Therefore, insofar as the risk assessment is concerned, there is no requirement to include maintenance type problems, as the purpose of the general risk assessment is to highlight risks likely to exist for a reasonable period of time. If maintenance risks were included in the risk assessment, it would be necessary to review the assessment at frequent, perhaps even daily intervals, in order to record the resolution of each outstanding item as it occurred. This is not to suggest that maintenance risks are not important. Indeed, close management of this kind of risk is essential to ensure that unacceptable delay does not occur in resolving them, as well as detecting undesirable trends in their frequency.

Regulation 4 – health and safety arrangements

2.7   The requirement of this regulation is for employers to develop and enforce arrangements which are appropriate, taking account of the size and nature of the business, for effectively planning, organising, controlling, monitoring and reviewing the preventative and protective measures to control risks.

There is similarity between this requirement and that of *regulation 2(3)* of the *Health and Safety at Work etc. Act 1974*, which requires every employer of more than four people to develop and publish a health and safety policy. In both cases the requirement to publish details applies if the workforce exceeds four.

A well considered and constructed health and safety policy should incorporate all of the requirements of *regulation 4* and if it does, there is no requirement to produce further separate documentation to satisfy this regulation. Where *regulation 4* has prompted the publication of additional documentation, this could be attached to the health and safety policy for completeness sake, although this will not be possible for larger organisations.

Whatever course of action is taken, it is important to ensure that there is sufficient evidence of arrangements covering each of the elements called for in *regulation 4*, namely planning, organisation, control, monitoring and review.

It should be noted that 'review' is included in this regulation as well as being a key requirement of risk management in *regulation 3(3)* of *MHSWR*.

Table 2 – The elements of arrangements for health and safety

Planning	Applying a systematic approach by setting objectives and identifying priorities. It is unlikely to be possible to do everything considered necessary at once, so those protective measures which will safeguard the greatest number should come first. Most risks can be eliminated at the outset when new facilities and equipment are contemplated, or minimised by using physical control measures or changing methods of working.
Organisation	Ensuring that the organisation structure is such that it is geared to progressive improvements in health and safety. *Regulation 6* of *MHSWR* calls for the appointment of a minimum of one competent health and safety adviser to assist employers in complying with their health and safety responsibilities. Advisers may be employees or consultants, or a combination of these. Health and safety advisers should contribute to the debate on the organisational arrangements for health and safety compliance.
Control	Making sure that procedures developed to improve health and safety are actually being complied with. This is an aspect of the arrangements which should be central to the health and safety advisers work.

Monitoring and review	Standards will fall if there is an indifferent monitoring regime. Monitoring must not be regarded as an occasional activity, to be carried out if there is a spare moment. Everyone in the organisation must be involved in some aspect of monitoring; they should know what they are expected to monitor, how often and with what result, and to whom they should send the monitoring report.

Regulation 5 – health surveillance

2.8   The requirement for health surveillance of employees will usually arise as a result of working with materials or substances subject to specific regulations, for example *COSHH*, Asbestos, Lead. In such cases the arrangements for health surveillance should already be in place. See Chapter 8.

In the event the (general) risk assessment also concludes that health surveillance is necessary to protect employees against a risk identified, the surveillance must be provided free of charge and take place during working hours.

Critical factors in determining whether to initiate a health surveillance programme are:

—   the possibility of an identifiable disease or adverse health condition related to the work activity, and a reasonable likelihood of that disease or condition occurring under the actual conditions of work;

—   the existence of recognised techniques for detecting indications of the disease or condition;

—   that the health surveillance programme will be beneficial in improving the protection of the employees potentially at risk.

An example of a workplace health risk which regular health checks would be unlikely to detect is Leptospirosis (Weil's Disease). This condition can occur due to exposure to the urine of rats, and is therefore a risk to which workers in sewers, tunnels and on or in inland waters are exposed. As the incubation period for the onset of this disease, and its duration once contracted are relatively short, detection of the disease as a result of a routine medical check would be rare.

Therefore the precautions recommended for workers potentially at risk from Weil's disease are strict hygiene, including washing/showering immediately after leaving a place where exposure could occur, and before eating, drinking or using toilet facilities. They should also carry a card which they should present to their GP in the event they manifest the influenza type symptoms characteristic of the disease.

Where health surveillance is contemplated, it is important to obtain advice from an appropriate medical source and those employees who are to be covered by the arrangements should have the opportunity to comment on the proposed frequency of examination or other medical procedures, as well as being allowed access to a suitably qualified medical practitioner for advice.

Once commenced, medical surveillance should be continued while the employee remains in employment, and an individual health record should be kept for each person in the surveillance programme. Employees must have access to their records, and regular communication of the results of surveillance is good practice; however such information must relate to groups of employees, and it should not be possible to identify any individual from the information provided.

It is sometimes necessary to include within a health surveillance programme, procedures for the detection of more than one adverse condition.

Regulation 6 – health and safety assistance

2.9   *Regulation 6* requires employers to appoint one or more competent health and safety advisers to advise them is respect to compliance with health and safety law and regulation. This requirement acknowledges the volume and complexity of health and safety law which employers have to comply with.

Clearly the contribution of competent advisers in respect to the development of suitable and sufficient risk assessments is essential, and this is discussed in Chapter 4 at paragraph 4.23.

Regulation 7 – procedures for serious and imminent danger and for danger areas

2.10   The requirements of this regulation are not novel, but they serve to remind employers of the importance of keeping these important safety arrangements under review and up to date.

The procedures must include fire precautions and the action to be taken in a fire emergency. Amendments to *regulation 3* (Risk Assessment) made in 1997 following the introduction of the *Fire*

2.11   Statutory Requirements for Risk Assessment

Precautions (Workplace) Regulations 1977 require most premises to specifically consider fire related risks in the general risk assessment, and this requirement will become universal during 1999.

Detailed information on the 'fire' risk assessment appear in Chapter 8 at paragraphs 8.64–8.66.

Regulation 8 – information for employees

2.11   The most important requirement of *regulation 8* is that of communicating to all employees in a 'comprehensible and relevant' manner, details of the risk assessment findings and the measures taken to remove or mitigate the risks identified. In addition they must also be given details of any risks which other employers or self-employed persons sharing the same premises have highlighted, if these risks have the propensity to affect them.

Employees must also be told about the procedures for dealing with serious and imminent danger and the identity of key staff appointed to ensure safe emergency evacuation of the premises.

The requirement for information provided under this regulation to be 'relevant and comprehensible' acknowledges the fact that there might be some among the workforce who either do not understand written English or who do not have English as their mother tongue. Where this is the case, special measures must be taken to impart this key information, and to ensure that it is fully understood. It follows from this that employers must keep a careful record of any employees who fall within the categories described, and to consider the risk posed by this fact in their risk assessment.

Regulation 9 – co-operation and co-ordination

2.12   Where employers and/or self-employed persons share a workplace, they must co-operate with each other in order to comply with all relevant health and safety requirements, especially those in respect to emergency evacuation.

They must also disclose to those with whom they share the premises details of any risks in their own risk assessment which could affect the employees of the others.

This was a novel requirement when *MHSWR* came into effect in January 1993, yet one which is most important in avoiding the possibility of confusion and exposure to danger in multi-occupancy premises, for example as a consequence of some occupants being unaware that evacuation is necessary, or that a bomb threat has been received, etc.

Any employer who shares a workplace with other employers or self-employed persons, and who has not been approached by those with whom he shares in respect to compliance with this regulation, should initiate dialogue with them to bring about compliance. If the building is managed by a landlord or agent, the approach should be made to them.

Tenants' committees are a useful vehicle for generating action to comply with *regulation 9*, for example by agreeing to the appointment of a health and safety co-ordinator to act on behalf of all occupants; it should not normally be necessary to appoint a health and safety co-ordinator where there is a landlord's agent.

Regulation 10 – persons working in host employers' or self-employed persons' undertakings

2.13 The purpose of this regulation is to ensure that persons who attend to do work at the premises of an employer other than their own employer, are provided with sufficient information to understand the risks to their health and safety while they are carrying out that work. Examples are contracting staff carrying out maintenance or alteration work, temporary staff seconded from an employment agency, etc.

Experience has shown that those working in the premises of a 'host' employer can be at risk, either because their own employer has not properly briefed them on the risks to which they could be exposed, or because the host employer has not considered it necessary to provide them with information about these risks, even though this risk information has been conveyed to his own employees. The multifatality Swan Hunter accident was a tragic example of such a failure.

The Swan Hunter case

The prosecution of shipyard owners Swan Hunter and a contractor employed indirectly on behalf of Swan Hunter (Telemeter Installations Ltd) arose as a consequence of a multi-fatality fire in September 1976 aboard HMS Glasgow – then undergoing a major refit at Swan Hunters Neptune Yard on the River Tyne.

Eight men employed by Telemeter Installations Ltd were killed in the fire as a consequence of a welder, without any negligence on his part, striking his arc with his welding torch.

The ensuing fire spread with alarming speed and ferocity due to the fact that the poorly ventilated internal hold of the warship, in which the men were working, had become dangerously oxygen enriched overnight due to failure to turn off the oxygen supply to a hose at the end of the previous evening's shift.

It was not disputed that a hose had been left overnight below decks and that the oxygen supply to it had not been turned off, contrary to written instructions on this matter appearing in Swan Hunter's 'Blue Book'; an employee of Telemeter was responsible for this failure.

Swan Hunter had experienced two earlier fatal fires as a result of oxygen enrichment, and were therefore well aware of the dangers. In order to avoid a repetition of such accidents, they had prepared and published a 'Blue Book' of instructions for users of fuel and oxygen.

Although the Blue Book was issued to employees of Swan Hunter, copies were not provided to the employees of other companies, including those of Telemeter, even though, in many cases, contractors employees worked alongside their own men.

Charges were brought as follows:

Swan Hunter – Sections 2 and 3 of *HSWA 1974*,

Telemeter Installations Ltd – Sections 2 and 3 of *HSWA 1974*.

Section 2 is concerned with the duties of employers to their own employees in respect to their health and safety, *Section 3* with the duties of employers to persons not being their employees whose health and safety could be affected by the conduct of the employers operations.

Telemeter pleaded guilty and Swan Hunter were found guilty by the Crown Court. Swan Hunter appealed.

The Court of Appeal Judge upheld the convictions, stating that is was entirely reasonably practicable for Swan Hunter, having developed and published instructions to safeguard employees working with fuel and oxygen, to have issued the same instructions to any contractors or sub-contractors who would be carrying out such work on their premises.

This case was noteworthy in that it was the first prosecution under *HSWA 1974* to be tried before a jury and the first in which the Court of Appeal had to consider the provisions of the *Health and Safety at Work etc. Act 1974*.

The principles established by this case still hold good, although the general requirement to consider the health and safety of non-employees on which the *HSWA section 3* charges were brought is now established more specifically in *regulation 3(1)(b)* of *MHSW 1992*, which calls for an employers risk assessment to take account of risks to the health and safety of persons not in their employment arising out of or in connection with the conduct by him of his undertaking.

Regulation 10 of *MHSW* is also germane to this situation. This requires host employers, *inter alia*, to provide non-employees working on their premises with details of any risks to their health and safety to which they could be exposed, and the measures which have been taken to remove or mitigate them.

Regulation 10 calls for the provision of information by host employers or self-employed persons to the employers of persons who will be coming to work on their premises, AND TO THE EMPLOYEES themselves, regarding risks that might affect them, the measures taken to manage those risks, and the arrangements to deal with emergencies, including identifying staff nominated to implement evacuation procedures.

By requiring this key information to be provided to employers AND their employees by the host employer, the regulation seeks to avoid a repetition of accidents similar to that at the Swan Hunter shipyard. All employers should ensure that their arrangements for providing information to comply with this regulation are properly documented and that monitoring is in place to ensure compliance.

Regulation 11 – capabilities and training

2.14 This requires employers to take account of the capabilities of employees as regards health and safety when entrusting tasks to them, and to provide adequate health and safety training to employees on being recruited and on being exposed to new or increased risks due to:

— being transferred or given a change of responsibilities;
— the introduction of new work equipment or a change in work equipment already in use;
— introduction of new technology;
— the introduction of a new system of work or a change in an existing system of work.

Training should be repeated where appropriate, take place during working hours, and be adapted to take account of any new or changed risks to the health and safety of the employees concerned.

Regulation 12 – employee's duties

2.15   Employees have important duties in relation to risk.

In addition to being required to use all work equipment as instructed, employees are required to report to their employer or persons nominated by the employer any instances of serious and imminent danger, or shortcoming in the health and safety arrangements that they become aware of and which could affect their health and safety at work

Regulations 13A–13C – risks to new or expectant mothers
regulation 13D – protection of young persons

2.16   Both these important regulations are discussed in detail in Chapter 7.

Summary

2.17   As the regulations described in this chapter are about the management of health and safety, they are by definition about the management of workplace risks. It is therefore essential that when developing a new risk assessment or reviewing an existing one, those involved take account not only of *regulation 3*, but of the other constituent regulations within *MHSWR* which have been described.

Quick reference checklist for Chapter 2: Statutory Requirements – Part 1

Requirements	Relevant Paragraphs
— Do adequate arrangements exist to demonstrate compliance with the requirement of *regulation 4* of *MHSWR*, i.e. planning, organising, controlling, monitoring and reviewing measures for managing risk?	2.7
— If your Health and Safety Policy is regarded as satisfying the *regulation 4* duty, is the H&S Policy endorsed to confirm this, and does the policy have provision on the cover or prominently to record the dates of review of the document, or at least the latest date of review?	2.7
— Is your health and safety adviser (or advisers) appointed formally, and does your H&S Policy show details of the adviser in Part II – organisation and responsibilities?	2.9
— If you share your work premises with others, is there full co-operation on all health and safety matters, in particular in respect to emergency procedures?	2.12
— Do you have an established procedure to ensure that all non-employees working on the premises are properly briefed on health and safety matters, in particular in respect to risks and emergency procedures?	2.13
— Do your training arrangements take account of the requirement to provide special health and safety training in the following circumstances: • when an employee is promoted; • when work equipment is modified or new equipment introduced; • when new technology is introduced; • when new systems of work are introduced or existing systems modified?	2.14

3 Statutory Requirements for Risk Assessment — Part 2

Introduction

3.1 Where health and safety regulations coming into force after 1992 include the requirement to assess risks pertaining to the subject of the regulations, and most do, they state that a risk assessment in compliance with *regulation 3* of *MHSWR* is necessary.

The most important of the regulations with this requirement in respect to risk assessment are discussed in Chapter 8, *Statutory Requirements for Risk Assessment – Part 3*.

Purpose of this chapter

3.2 This chapter is concerned with two important regulations which were introduced at the same time as the *Management of Health and Safety at Work Regulations* (1 January 1993), but which do not follow the pattern of the regulations described in paragraph 1, instead calling for a method of risk assessment unique to them. These are the *Health and Safety (Display Screen Equipment) Regulations 1992* (*DSE*) and the *Manual Handling Operations Regulations 1992* (*MHO*).

For both regulations, there is official guidance on the documentation to be used for the assessment process, and also customised forms for the purpose.

Although a model assessment form for manual handling was incorporated into the guidance to the *MHO regulations*, and appears again in the revised guidance published in November 1998, the HSE did not produce a model assessment form for DSE assessment until 1994, and then as a 'stand alone' document, copies of which can be purchased from HSE Books. Samples of DSE workstation assessment forms appear as appendices at the end of this chapter.

The *Health and Safety (Display Screen Equipment) Regulations 1992* (*DSE*)

Introduction and background

3.3 These regulations, together with five others concerned with aspects of workplace health and safety, became effective on 1

January 1993, the first day of the European Single Market. Of these six regulations only the *Display Screen Equipment Regulations* were unique in that they covered a workplace activity not previously addressed in legislation, whereas the other five regulations were variations or nuances of health and safety legislation already in existence here.

The *DSE regulations* appeared at a time when the use of display screen equipment (at that time more commonly referred to in the UK as 'VDUs') was growing very fast.

Concurrent with this mushrooming of use, anxiety about the potentially harmful effects of such work was increasing, no doubt fuelled by a number of successful claims for compensation brought by workers in the US and Australia for ill-health conditions arising from their work with DSE. Most common of these conditions was that known as RSI (Repetitive Strain Injury), now renamed at the behest of the medical profession WRULD (Work Related Upper Limb Disorder) in order to describe the condition more accurately, and recognising that variations of it can affect workers in a number of disparate occupations/industries.

Among the other health concerns expressed was the possibility of danger to pregnant women and/or their unborn children due to electromagnetic radiation emanating from display screens.

In the case of WRULD it is now accepted that the condition can arise when working with DSE if the correct posture – in particular the positions of the hands – is not adopted and maintained when keying, and recent legal judgements suggest that WRULD/RSI will become a recognised workplace injury.

The HSE and other workplace health organisations, contend that the danger from radiation is no greater than would arise from watching television or that present in almost all spheres of human activity. However, the fears that have been expressed, and the successful claims for compensation for ill-health associated with working with DSE – including some notable cases in the UK – drive home the message that employers must carry out DSE related 'workstation assessments' assiduously, and carefully follow-up any concerns expressed by DSE users to ensure that where such concerns are well founded, appropriate remedial or corrective action is taken.

When compensation is sought through the courts by employees alleging ill-health conditions precipitated by their work with DSE, their employer will need to be able to demonstrate compliance with the requirements of these regulations as evidence that they have not been negligent.

3.4 Statutory Requirements for Risk Assessment

If they have been dilatory in respect to assessing or re-assessing workstations, taking action where problems have been identified, or in respect to providing training, ensuring that breaks from DSE work are taken and making provision for free eye tests, this may prejudice the employers position.

Employers duties under DSE

3.4 The duties of employers under the *DSE regulations* can be summarised as follows:

(a) identifying those employees who are 'users';

(b) providing users with training in the requirements of the regulations;

(c) making provision for eye or eyesight tests for their employees designated as users, and where appropriate providing or making a contribution to the provision of 'special corrective appliances' where these are prescribed solely on account of the employees work with DSE;

(d) recognising the importance of users taking breaks away from their work with DSE;

(e) carrying out assessments of all user workstations against criteria set out in the *DSE regulations*;

(f) reviewing workstation assessments and addressing user concerns which are justified and capable of resolution;

(g) communicating details of all actions taken or planned to resolve the concerns of users highlighted by the individual workstation assessment or at other times;

(h) ensuring that re-assessment of a workstation takes place if the 'status quo' at that workstation alters.

Discussion of employers duties

(i) Identifying users

3.5 Not all workers required to use DSE are necessarily 'users' in the context of the *DSE regulations*. A 'user' is someone who habitually uses DSE as a significant part of their normal work.

Table 1 shows examples of occupations that definitely confer user status, others that depend upon the circumstances, and those which definitely are *not* users.

Table 1 Users and non-users of DSE

Part 1

Criteria for establishing whether a person is a DSE 'user' for the purpose of the DSE regulations.

The criteria below do not have to be applied slavishly, and in any event are subjective. However, if most or all of the criteria do apply, the person concerned should be classified as a 'user'

- the individual has to use display screen equipment to do their work – there are no alternative ways of doing it which achieve the same standards;
- the individual has no discretion, they are required to work with DSE;
- there is a requirement for specific training and/or skills in the use of DSE in order to do the job;
- the work routine entails work with DSE continually for periods of an hour or more at a time, and
- this is the general pattern of use most days;
- an important requirement of the job is fast transfer of information between the individual and the screen;
- the standards of performance for the job in question require high levels of concentration and attention to detail, and the consequences of mistakes may be serious.

Part 2

A non-exhaustive list of jobs involving work with display screens.

This list is an indicator only, and does not mean that everyone in the job categories shown is or is not a 'user' as the case may be. Final determination of 'user' status or otherwise, particularly in borderline cases, may require a detailed risk assessment to be carried out in order to ensure all the relevant factors are taken into account.

a) Definitely 'users'

— word processing pool workers engaged full-time in text input;
— full-time secretaries using all the electronic equipment associated with a modern office;
— journalists and news sub-editors;
— operators involved in tele-sales, complaints, order processing and tracking, directory enquiries, reference librarians;
— air traffic controllers, finance house dealers, graphic designers.

b) Possibly 'users'

— client managers;
— building society customer support officers;
— airline check-in clerks; and
— others whose use of DSE, while frequent, is usually for short periods at a time.
— However, persons falling into this category, if currently not classified as 'users', can quickly qualify for user status if their workload increases. Therefore it is important not only to keep the situation under review, but to instruct non-users to highlight at once any marked upturn in DSE work.

3.5 Statutory Requirements for Risk Assessment

Table 1 *continued*

c) Definitely not 'users'

— Senior managers;
— receptionists;
— maintenance and security staff where their work entails irregular and short duration reference to DSE monitors, and whose use of keyboards is minimal.

Table 1 notwithstanding, many employers opt to confer 'user' status on all their staff who do work involving the use of DSE, irrespective of whether such work is significant or habitual. There is nothing to prevent this, indeed it confers rights on those so designated, for example the right to eye or eyesight tests, breaks away from the work, etc.

(ii) Providing users with training

It is essential that all users receive a period of initial training in relation to DSE and if not already received, basic health and safety training. The DSE training should cover the importance of good posture and ergonomic practice, details of eye test arrangements, the importance of taking breaks away from DSE work at intervals, the assessment process – in particular the standards which should be achieved in terms of workstation conditions (hardware, software, furniture and the working environment).

This training should take place *before* the workstation assessment is carried out. All existing users, and any person who it is intended should become a user, should receive the training, details of which, including the names of those attending, should be documented and the record retained.

(iii) Eye and eyesight tests

Employees are entitled to eye and eyesight tests as follows:

— on first becoming a user, or if it is intended that they are to become users;

— following the first test, further tests at intervals recommended by the optician carrying out the initial test – usually every two years; or

— at any other time that a user believes that their eyesight or general health is being affected by their work with DSE.

NB: It is emphasised that although employees have a right to these

26

tests, it is NOT a duty. Employees wishing to exercise their right to an eye test should therefore ask for one.

Special Corrective Appliances

If the optician carrying out the eye test concludes that special corrective appliances (glasses or contact lenses) are necessary *solely* due to a users work with DSE, their employer must pay for these in addition to paying for the eye tests. However, employers are only obliged to pay a sum equivalent to the cost of providing normal glasses through the health service.

(iv) Breaks away from working with DSE

It is important that breaks away from work with DSE, especially use of the keyboard, are taken before the onset of fatigue, and that frequent breaks of short duration are preferable to a routine of longer breaks at fixed intervals. Breaks should ideally be a mixture of rest breaks and periods when other non-DSE work is undertaken, for example filing, making telephone calls, attending meetings, etc.

Managers should understand the importance of their staff taking breaks, and be vigilant to ensure that no user is placed under such production related pressure that they work for long periods without taking breaks. It has been proved that uninterrupted work with DSE for several hours at a time is a prime cause of strain and other ill-health conditions.

(v) Assessment of user workstations

Workstation assessment is pivotal to compliance with the DSE regulations, and must be undertaken in respect to every workstation where work is being carried out on behalf of the employer by DSE users.

The purpose of the assessment is to identify any risks to users which are posed by their use of the workstation, and, so far as is reasonably practicable, to remove or mitigate these risks.

Those who are responsible for the management of the DSE assessment programme must be suitably trained and experienced.

(vi) Workstation assessors

Workstation assessors should have the ability to:

— assess risks arising from the workstation and the kind of display screen work being carried out;

— draw upon additional sources of information on risk as necessary;

— draw valid and reliable conclusions from the assessment; of risks associated with the work with DSE;

— make clear records of assessments and communicate the findings to those who are required to take action to address them;

— recognise their own limitations, and seek help by calling on such other expertise as is necessary.

(vii) Responding to the concerns of 'users'

The assessment itself cannot be undertaken for any workstation without the user of that workstation being present; this rule applies even if every workstation in an area is identical in design and layout.

Anthroprometric studies have shown that there are significant numbers of people who are either below or above what is deemed to be an average shape and size.

In terms of DSE workstations such people are entitled to be provided with any aids necessary to ensure that they are comfortable when using their workstation. For example, a shorter person, having made all the adjustments necessary to their chair in relation to the work surface height in order to ensure that there is a horizontal plane between their elbow, finger tips and keyboard, might find that this has resulted in them being unable to place both feet flat to the ground without causing strain/discomfort to the backs of their legs and their thighs, or by pointing their toes to the ground.

In such cases, it will be necessary for them to be provided with a suitable footrest. These and other problems related to the relationship between individuals and their working environment (ergonomics) mean that assessment of workstations cannot take place without each user being present and having the opportunity to comment on their own situation. Therefore any employer who has developed workstation assessments in the absence of those who work at the workstations has *not* complied with the letter or spirit of the regulations.

Paragraph 8 describes the appendices to this chapter, which include, *inter alia*, the various elements to be covered when carrying out a DSE workstation assessment.

(viii) Reviewing workstation assessments and addressing user concerns which are justified and capable of resolution

Not everything that a user has concerns about can be addressed to their satisfaction; the qualifying condition in these regulations, as with most health and safety related requirements, is whether it is 'reasonably practicable' to carry out the measures being considered, or indeed to contemplate *any* remedial measures.

Inevitably there are some individuals who will complain about every aspect of their workplace; the skill required of those managing the assessment programme is that of separating the genuine and justified concern from the trivial and inconsequential. Even in an organisation who have provided the best and most advanced furniture and equipment, there will be some users who are not 100 per cent satisfied.

(ix) Actions following assessment

However conscientiously employers apply themselves to resolving problems highlighted by DSE users during the assessment process, or indeed at any other time that users raise issues or concerns, the benefits from these actions will not be fully optimised unless they are complemented by timely and positive feed-back.

Individually users want to know what is gong to be done (or not done as the case may be) about the concerns which they have raised during the workstation assessments process, or at any other time that they have problems relating to their work with DSE. Collectively users expect to receive feed-back on the programme as a whole. How many new chairs, foot-rests etc. have been provided? What percentage of users experienced glare on monitor screens, or problems with the air conditioning and so on ...

Nothing does more to destroy the credibility of a new programme or initiative than that it starts in a blaze of publicity, enjoins employees to co-operate fully to make it a success and then dissolves into silence.

(x) Re-assessment

A DSE workstation assessment, when completed, can only be of use while the workstation in question remains as it was at the time the assessment was carried out. As soon as the 'status quo' changes, the validity of the assessment may cease and a fresh workstation assessment is required.

3.5 Statutory Requirements for Risk Assessment

Given the dynamic nature of many organisations, the need for re-assessment may arise on a number of occasions during the lifetime of a workstation. Unless arrangements exist to carry out re-assessment whenever significant changes occur, there is, *prima facie*, a breach of these regulations, possibly accompanied by an increased risk of ill-health conditions and claims for compensation arising from these conditions.

The following changes in a workstation necessitate re-assessment of all or part of an existing assessment:

— a major change in the software used;

— a major change in the hardware (screen, keyboard, input devices, etc.);

— a major change in the workstation furniture;

— a substantial increase in the amount of time required to be spent using DSE;

— a substantial change in other task requirements involving DSE, e.g. more speed or accuracy called for;

— if the workstation is relocated;

— if the lighting is significantly modified;

— if research findings have identified a significant new risk or showed that a recognised hazard should be re-evaluated.

In respect to the last item, at least two significant developments in respect to work with DSE have occurred which, if relevant, should be taken into account and might require a review of part or all of an existing workstation assessment: new thinking in respect to the position of the monitor screen in relation to the line of sight of a user, and the introduction and widespread use of the mouse.

At the time the *DSE regulations* came into force, the recommended height of the monitor screen was such that it enabled the users eyes to fall upon the screen approximately 33 per cent of the distance down from its top, with the user sitting upright and staring directly ahead. This advice still holds good for touch typists. However, for those who are not touch typists, and therefore have an equal need to look down at the keyboard, it is sensible for the monitor screen to be lower down so that the focus of the eye of those who cannot touch type is not constantly having to alternate between a keyboard at desk top level and a screen at a much higher level.

The advent of the mouse has created new challenges in terms of posture and ergonomics, which if not addressed, have the potential to cause problems, particularly WRULD. These can occur if the mouse is kept at arms length, especially to one side, or the hand clutches the mouse instead of resting palm down on it or immediately in line with it, so that the fingers are extended, not clenched. Ideally the mouse should be close into the body to avoid unnecessary stretching.

Importance of views of users

3.6   The forms designed for workstation assessments usually omit to provide space for users to explain more fully what they mean when they indicate by a tick or cross that they are not satisfied, or to describe any concerns about their work with DSE which is not covered by any of the questions on the assessment form.

Employers should ensure that their DSE assessors are briefed to give users the opportunity to raise any other issues they have concerning DSE work, or to provide sufficient paper for written comments to be made and attached to the assessment form used, if the forms do not include space for this purpose.

DSE and risk assessment

3.7   The *DSE* regulations, in calling for an assessment to be carried out in respect to every DSE user workstation, are in effect requiring a risk assessment confined to risks associated with working with DSE.

The regulations themselves highlight all the risks, and in most cases the remedial measures required, by including in their associated schedules requirements and guidance on minimum standards to be achieved in complying with them. Further assistance is also provided by the HSE model assessment form, which includes all the questions which need to be asked to satisfy the requirements of the regulations.

Appendices

3.8   The appendices relating to the *DSE regulations* that follow are:

Appendix A – Minimum requirements for workstations
Appendix B – Guidance on the requirements in Appendix B
Appendix C – Possible effects on health from DSE work

3.9 Statutory Requirements for Risk Assessment

Appendix D – HSE version of DSE assessment form
Appendix E – Example of a typical DSE assessment form
Appendix F – Form recording action to be taken in respect to negative responses by users during workstation assessment.
Appendix G – DSE summary sheet.

The Manual Handling Operations Regulations 1992 (MHO)

Introduction

3.9 These regulations came into effect on 1 January 1993, together with five other health and safety regulations, including those in respect to working with display screen equipment, which is the subject of the first part of this chapter.

In respect to risk assessment, the *MHO regulations* have similarity to those for DSE in that the hierarchy of measures to address risks associated with manual handling and the documentation of the process of assessment are explained in the regulations or the official guidance to them, hence their inclusion in this chapter which discusses regulations calling for risk assessment to be carried out using a different approach to that outlined in the primary regulations concerned with this subject – *regulation 3* of *MHSWR*.

Despite differences in the manner of dealing with risks as described above, initial identification of the existence of potential risks in connection with manual handling should normally arise as part of the 'general' risk identification process within *regulation 3* of *MHSWR*.

Manual handling at work is the most common cause of absence, ill-health or injury and the introduction of regulations focusing specifically on the subject were necessary.

No weight maxima specified

3.10 Although the objective of the regulations is to bring about a significant reduction in health problems associated with manual handling, they do not stipulate maximum weights for handling carried out by humans; this is because it is considered that the weight of loads being handled is only one of many factors that are relevant. The range of factors that should be taken into account are scheduled in Appendix H.

What does manual handling mean?

3.11   Manual handling is the transporting or supporting of a load (including humans and animals), and involving lifting, putting down, pushing, pulling, carrying or moving thereof by hand or bodily force.

Employers duties

3.12   The duties of employers under these regulations can be summarised as follows:

— avoid manual handling work so far as is reasonably practicable;

— assess all manual handling operations that cannot be avoided; and

— reduce the risk of injury as far as is reasonably practicable

Table 2 is a flow chart showing the manual handling risk assessment process.

Avoiding manual handling work

3.13   Many workplace manual handling operations have become so much a part of the ongoing routine that nobody has considered whether they could be eliminated altogether.

Examples

— Processes where product reaches the end of a conveyor belt and then has to be manually removed and taken to a packing bench or area. If packing or packaging is incorporated into the process, when the product reaches the end of the belt it is packed ready for storage and/or despatch by machinery. A further improvement to this arrangement would be the use of fork lift trucks to remove the packaged product and takes it to despatch or stores as appropriate.

— The movement of patients, even when transported on hospital trolleys, still entails potentially injurious manual handling. In some circumstances it will be less onerous to bring the treatment process to the patient rather than taking the patient to the treatment.

— Discharging parcels/packages from the guards van of a train onto a station platform means that someone has to pick up the

3.13 Statutory Requirements for Risk Assessment

Table 2 Manual handling risk assessment process

Regulations 2(1)

Do the Regulations apply – ie does the work involve manual handling operations?	**No** →

Regulation 4(1)(a)   **Yes** ↓

Is there a risk of injury?	**No** →

Yes/possibly ↓

Is it reasonable practicable to avoid moving the loads?	**Yes** →

No ↓

Is it reasonably practicable to automate or mechanise the operation?	**Yes** ↓

Does some risk of *manual handling* injury remain?	**No** →

No ↓   **Yes/possibly** ↓

Regulation 4(1)(b)(i)

Carry out manual handling assessment

Regulation 4(1)(b)(ii/iii)

Determine measures to reduce risk of injury to the lowest level reasonably practicable

↓

Implement the appropriate measures

↓

Evaluate the effects. Are the risk controlled as planned?	**Yes** →

No ↓

End of initial exercise

↓

Review if conditions change significantly

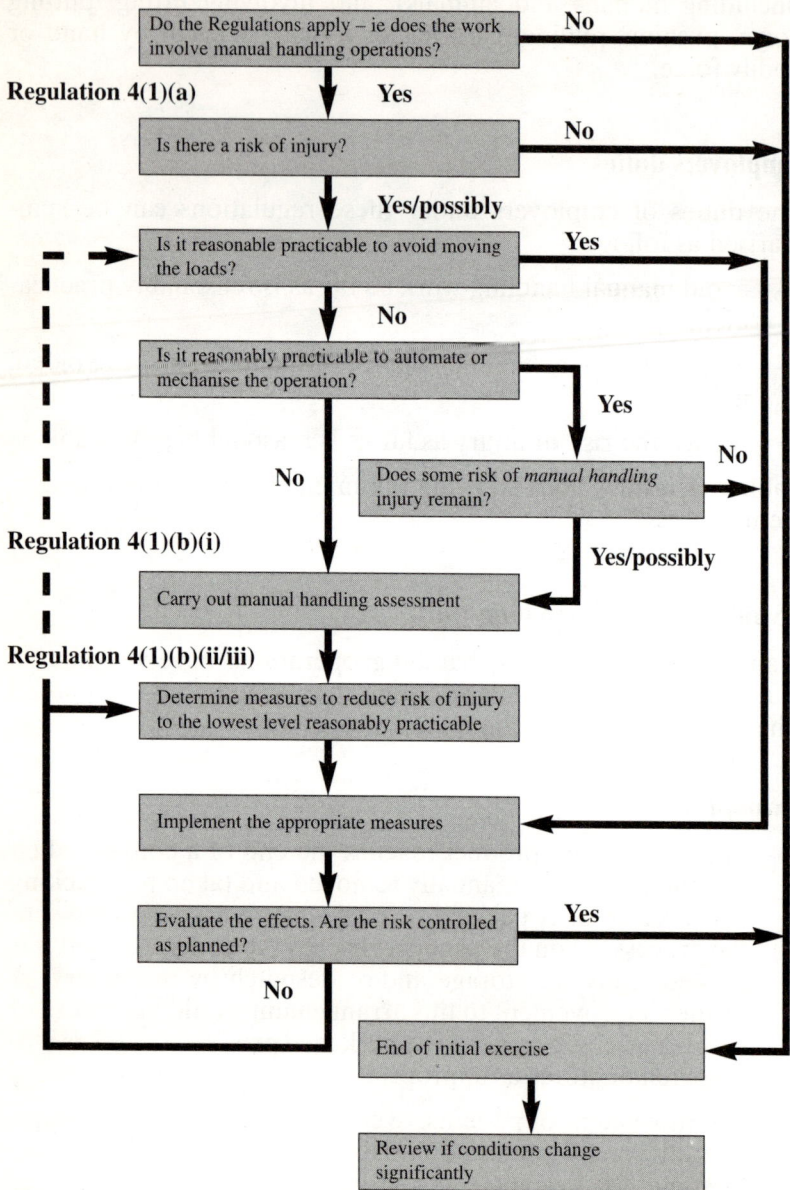

packages and put them onto a trolley for moving; this could be avoided by pre-positioned trolleys so that packages can be transferred directly from train to trolley.

Alternatives to manual handling

3.14 Although mechanical and electronic aids to reduce the amount of manual handling being undertaken are increasingly used, there is still a very high incidence of avoidable manual handling. Cost of equipment is a factor that militates against the introduction of machinery, yet the *MHO regulations* make clear that such aids should be made available unless it can be shown that the cost versus risk balance is grossly disproportionate.

Minimising the strain in manual handling

3.15 Even if it is impossible to avoid some human involvement in handling, there are ways of minimising the risks to health, for example:

— breaking down loads into smaller units. For example copying paper in boxes can be split into constituent packages, drinking water containers of 13 litre capacity can be introduced in place of heavier containers;

— instructing suppliers to deliver to the place of storage or of use rather than at a 'goods inwards' point, thus avoiding double handling;

— storing heavier items at or below waist level and not at heights which would require those handling the items to stretch above shoulder height;

— emphasising that no individual should try to lift weights that they consider to be beyond their capacity;

— providing initial and refresher manual handling (Kinetic) training, both theoretical and practical, to all employees who may be required to undertake manual handling.

Responsibilities of employees

3.16 It is important that the training of employees emphasises the importance of their contribution to ensuring absence of risk to health when manual handling. For example:

— when carrying out work involving manual handling, doing so in accordance with the training they have received;

— in particular, not attempting to handle anything which they believe could be injurious to them;

— using all the mechanical/electronic aids provided to assist them;

— reporting immediately to their supervisor any temporary or permanent health condition which might affect their ability to carry out manual handling tasks.

The process of manual handling assessment and relevant documentation

3.17   The appendices to this part of Chapter 3 provide all the information necessary to carry out and record assessments to comply with the *Manual Handling Operations Regulations*.

These are:

Appendix H – basic principles of safe manual handling
Appendix I   – the five key factors which must be considered when making manual handling assessment – the task, the loads, the working environment, individual capability and 'other factors'
Appendix J   – manual handling risk assessment – detailed assessment guidelines filter
Appendix K – example of an assessment checklist and its application to a manual handling risk

Quick reference checklist for Chapter 3:
Statutory Requirements for Risk Assessment — Part 2

Requirements	Relevant Paragraphs
Display Screen Equipment	
— Is there clear identification of staff (or jobs) determined as having DSE 'User' status and those that do not?	3.4(i) 3.5(i)
— Do your arrangements for compliance with the DSE regulations include as a minimum all the items covered by paragraph 3.4?	3.4
— Are you satisfied that those responsible for assessing DSE workstations are competent to do so?	3.4 3.5(v)
— Do all 'users' understand the company arrangements for eye tests and rules pertaining to the provision of 'special corrective appliances' (glasses/contact lenses)?	3.5(iii)
— Do all users understand that the request for an eye test must come from them – and that such tests are entirely voluntary?	3.5(iii)
— Do all managers recognise the importance of users taking regular rest breaks?	3.5(iv)
— Do all users receive a period of training on the DSE regulations *before* co-operating with the assessment of their workstation?	3.5(ii)
— Do arrangements exist to ensure follow-up reporting to every DSE user who has raised issues or requested additional items, e.g. footrest, document holder during or since their workstation assessment?	3.5(vii)
— Have sufficient resources been allocated and do procedures make clear that re-assessment of a DSE workstation must be made whenever the 'status quo' changes?	3.5(viii)
Manual Handling	
— Do your arrangements for compliance with the Manual Handling Operations Regulations include as a minimum the matters covered by paragraph 3.12?	3.12
— In particular are you satisfied that all the mechanical aids to handling that it is reasonable to introduce have been obtained?	3.14
— Is kinetic handling training provided for all staff whose work entails or is likely to include manual handling?	3.15
— Are managers and supervisors in areas where manual handling takes place vigilant in enforcing the use of mechanical and other aids to handling which have been introduced?	3.15
— If a statutory inspector asked to see the manual handling risk assessment for your operations, would this pose a problem?	3.12

3.17   Statutory Requirements for Risk Assessment

List of Appendices – Chapter 3

Display Screen Regulations

A – Minimum requirements for workstations
B – Guidance on the requirements for workstations
C – Possible effects on health from DSE work
D – HSE version of DSE assessment form
E – Example of a typical DSE assessment form
F – Form recording action to be taken in respect to negative responses by users during workstation assessment (recommended that this form is attached to every workstation assessment)
G – DSE summary sheet (used to summarise the results of individual DSE assessments – useful when presenting status and results of a DSE assessment programme)

Manual Handling Regulations

H – Basic principles of safe manual handling
I – Five key factors
J – Manual handling risk assessment – detailed assessment guidelines filter
K – Assessment checklist example

Appendix A – Minimum requirements for workstation

(Which sets out the minimum requirements for workstations which are contained in the Annex to Council Directive 90/270/EEC[a] on the minimum safety and health requirements for work with display screen equipment)

Extent to which employers must ensure that workstations meet the requirements laid down in this Schedule

1   An employer shall ensure that a workstation meets the requirements laid down in this Schedule to the extent that –

(a)   those requirements relate to a component which is present in the workstation concerned;

(b)   those requirements have effect with a view to securing the health, safety and welfare of persons at work; and

(c)   the inherent characteristics of a given task make compliance with those requirements appropriate as respects the workstation concerned.

Equipment

2   (a)   *General comment*

The use as such of the equipment must not be a source of risk for operators or users.

(b)   *Display screen*

The characters on the screen shall be well-defined and clearly formed, of adequate size and with adequate spacing between the characters and lines.

The image on the screen should be stable, with no flickering or other forms of instability.

The brightness and the contrast between the characters and the background shall be easily adjustable by the operator or user, and also be easily adjustable to ambient conditions.

The screen must swivel and tilt easily and freely to suit the needs of the operator or user.

It shall be possible to use a separate base for the screen or an adjustable table.

The screen shall be free of reflective glare and reflections liable to cause discomfort to the operator or user.

(c)   *Keyboard*

The keyboard shall be tiltable and separate from the screen so as to allow the operator or user to find a comfortable working position avoiding fatigue in the arms or hands.

The space in front of the keyboard shall be sufficient to provide support for the hands and arms of the operator or user.

The keyboard shall have a matt surface to avoid reflective glare.

The arrangement of the keyboard and the characteristics of the keys shall be such as to facilitate the use of the keyboard.

The symbols on the keys shall be adequately contrasted and legible from the design working position.

(d)   *Work desk or work surface*

The work desk or work surface shall have a sufficiently large, low-reflectance surface and allow a flexible arrangement of the screen, keyboard, documents and related equipment.

The document holder shall be stable and adjustable and shall be positioned so as to minimise the need for uncomfortable head and eye movements.

There shall be adequate space for operators or users to find a comfortable position.

(e)   *Work chair*

The work chair shall be stable and allow the operator or user easy freedom of movement and a comfortable position.

The seat shall be adjustable in height.

The seat back shall be adjustable in both height and tilt.

A footrest shall be made available to any operator or user who wishes one.

Environment

3   (a)   *Space requirements*

The workstation shall be dimensioned and designed so as to provide sufficient space for the operator or user to change position and vary movements.

(b)   *Lighting*

Any room lighting or task lighting provided shall ensure satisfactory lighting conditions and an appropriate contrast between the screen and the background environment, taking into account the type of work and the vision requirements of the operator or user.

Possible disturbing glare and reflections on the screen or other equipment shall be prevented by co-ordinating workplace and workstation layout with the positioning and technical characteristics of the artificial light sources.

(c)   *Reflections and glare*

Workstations shall be so designed that sources of light, such as windows and other openings, transparent or translucent walls, and brightly coloured fixtures or walls cause no direct glare and no distracting reflections on the screen.

Windows shall be fitted with a suitable system of adjustable covering to attenuate the daylight that falls on the workstation.

(d) *Noise*

Noise emitted by equipment belonging to any workstation shall be taken into account when a workstation is being equipped, with a view in particular to ensuring that attention is not distracted and speech is not disturbed.

(e) *Heat*

Equipment belonging to any workstation shall not produce excess heat which could cause discomfort to operators or users.

(f) *Radiation*

All radiation with the exception of the visible part of the electromagnetic spectrum shall be reduced to negligible levels from the point of view of the protection of operators' or users' health and safety.

(g) *Humidity*

An adequate level of humidity shall be established and maintained.

Interface between computer and operator/user

4   In designing, selecting, commissioning and modifying software, and in designing tasks using display screen equipment, the employer shall take into account the following principles:

(a) software must be suitable for the task;

(b) software must be easy to use and, where appropriate, adaptable to the level of knowledge or experience of the operator or user; no quantitative or qualitative checking facility may be used without the knowledge of the operators or users;

(c) systems must provide feedback to operators or users on the performance of those systems;

(d) systems must display information in a format and at a pace which are adapted to operators or users;

3.17 Statutory Requirements for Risk Assessment

Subjects dealt with in this Schedule

1 ADEQUATE LIGHTING
2 ADEQUATE CONTRAST, NO GLARE OR DISTRACTING REFLECTIONS
3 DISTRACTING NOISE MINIMISED
4 LEG ROOM AND CLEARANCES TO ALLOW POSTURAL CHANGES
5 WINDOW COVERING
6 SOFTWARE: APPROPRIATE TO TASK, ADAPTED TO USER, PROVIDES FEEDBACK ON SYSTEM STATUS, NO UNDISCLOSED MONITORING
7 SCREEN: STABLE IMAGE, ADJUSTABLE, READABLE, GLARE/ REFLECTION FREE
8 KEYBOARD: USABLE, ADJUSTABLE, DETACHABLE, LEGIBLE
9 WORK SURFACE: ALLOW FLEXIBLE ARRANGEMENTS, SPACIOUS, GLARE FREE
10 WORK CHAIR: ADJUSTABLE
11 FOOTREST

Seating and posture for typical office tasks

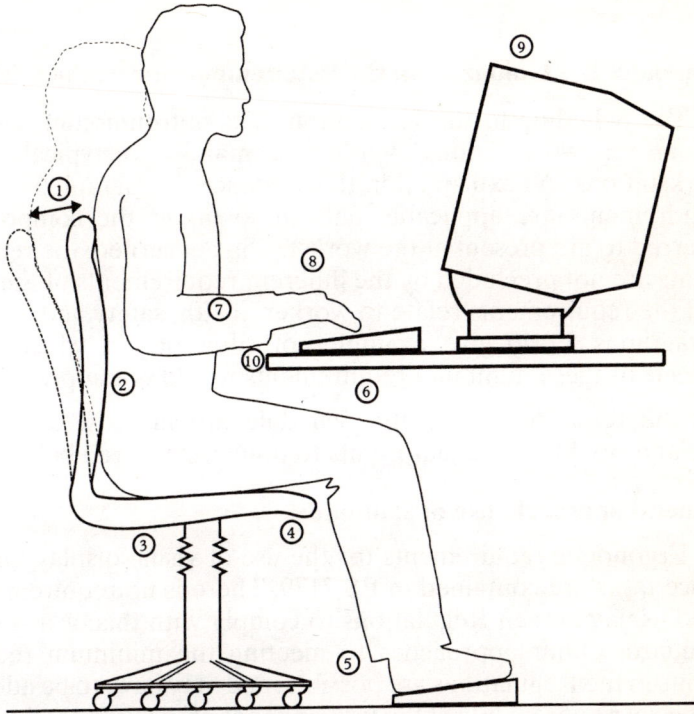

1 SEAT BACK ADJUSTABILITY
2 GOOD LUMBAR SUPPORT
3 SEAT HEIGHT ADJUSTABILITY
4 NO EXCESS PRESSURE ON UNDERSIDE OF THIGHS AND BACKS
  OF KNEES
5 FOOT SUPPORT IF NEEDED
6 SPACE FOR POSTURAL CHANGE, NO OBSTACLES UNDER DESK
7 FOREARMS APPROXIMATELY HORIZONTAL
8 MINIMAL EXTENSION, FLEXION OR DEVIATION OF WRISTS
9 SCREEN HEIGHT AND ANGLE SHOULD ALLOW
  COMFORTABLE HEAD POSITION
10 SPACE IN FRONT OF KEYBOARD TO SUPPORT HANDS/WRISTS
  DURING PAUSES IN KEYING

(e)   the principles of software ergonomics must be applied, in particular to human data processing.

Appendix B – Guidance on the requirements for workstations

1   The Schedule to the Regulations sets out minimum requirements for workstations, applicable mainly to typical office workstations. As explained in the guidance (paragraph 38) these requirements are applicable only in so far as the components referred to are present at the workstation concerned, the requirements are not precluded by the inherent requirements of the task, and the requirements relate to worker health, safety and welfare. Paragraphs 39–40 give examples of situations in which some aspects of these minimum requirements would not apply.

2   The requirements of the Schedule are in most cases self-explanatory but particular points to note are covered below.

General approach: use of standards

3   Ergonomic requirements for the use of visual display units in office tasks are contained in BS 7179. There is no requirement in the Display Screen Regulations to comply with this or any other standard. Other approaches to meeting the minimum requirements in the Regulations are possible, and may have to be adopted if special requirements of the task or needs of the user preclude the use of equipment made to relevant standards. However, employers may find standards helpful as workstations satisfying BS 7179, or forthcoming international standards (see below), would meet and in most cases go beyond the minimum requirements in the Schedule to the Regulations.

4   BS 7179 is a six-part interim standard covering the ergonomics of design and use of visual display terminals in offices; it is concerned with the efficient use of VDUs as well as with user health, safety and comfort. BS 7179 has been issued by the British Standards Institution in recognition of industry's immediate need for guidance and is intended for the managers and supervisors of VDU users as well as for equipment manufacturers. While originally confined to office VDU tasks, many of the general ergonomic recommendations in BS 7179 will be relevant to some non-office situations.

5   International standards are in preparation that will cover the same subject in an expanded form. BS 7179 will be withdrawn when the European standards organisation CEN (Comité Europeén de Normalisation) issues its multipart standard (EN

29241) concerned with the ergonomics of design and use of visual display terminals for office tasks. This CEN Standard will in turn be based on an ISO Standard (ISO 9241) that is currently being developed. The eventual ISO and CEN standards will cover screen and keyboard design and evaluation, workstation design and environmental requirements, non-keyboard input devices and ergonomic requirements for software design and usability. While the CEN standard is not formally linked to the Display Screen Equipment directive, one of its aims is to establish appropriate levels of user health and safety and comfort. Technical data in the various parts of the CEN standard (and currently BS 7179) may therefore help employers to meet the requirements laid down in the Schedule to the Regulations.

6 There are other standards that deal with requirements for furniture, some of which are cross-referenced by BS 7179. These include BS 3044, which is a guide to ergonomic principles in the design and selection of office furniture generally. There is also now a separate standardisation initiative within CEN concerned with the performance requirements for office furniture, including dimensioning appropriate for European user populations. Details of relevant British, European and international standards can be obtained from the Department of Trade and Industry – see Annex C.

7 Other more detailed and stringent standards are relevant to certain specialised applications of display screens, especially those where the health or safety of persons other than the screen user may be affected. Some examples in particular subject areas are:–

(1) *Process control*

  A large number of British and international standards are or will be relevant to the design of display screen interfaces for use in process control – such as the draft Standard ISO 11064 on the general ergonomic design of control rooms.

(2) *Applications with machinery safety implications*

  Draft Standard pr EN 614 pt 1 – Ergonomic design principles in safety of machinery.

(3) *Safety of programmable electronic systems*

  Draft document IEC 65A (Secretariat) 122 Draft: Functional safety of electrical/electronic programmable systems.

Applications such as these are outside the scope of these guidance notes. Anyone involved in the design of such display screen interfaces and others where there may be safety considerations for

non-users should seek appropriate specialist advice. Many relevant standards are listed in the DTI publication *Directory of HCI
Standards* – see Annex C.

Equipment

Display screen

8   Choice of display screen should be considered in relation to
other elements of the work system, such as the type and amount of
information required for the task, and environmental factors. A
satisfactory display can be achieved by custom design for a specific
task or environment, or by appropriate adjustments to adapt the
display to suit changing requirements or environmental conditions.

Display stability

9   Individual perceptions of screen flicker vary and a screen
which is flicker-free to 90% of users should be regarded as satisfying the minimum requirement. (It is not technically feasible to
eliminate flicker for all users). A change to a different display can
resolve individual problems with flicker. Persistent display
instabilities – flicker, jump, jitter or swim – may indicate basic
design problems and assistance should be sought from suppliers.

Brightness and contrast

10   Negative or positive image polarity (light characters on a dark
background, dark characters on a light background respectively) is
acceptable, and each has different advantages. With negative
polarity flicker is less perceptible, legibility is better for those with
low acuity vision, and characters may be perceived as larger than
they are; with positive polarity, reflections are less perceptible,
edges appear sharper and luminance balance is easier to achieve.

11   It is important for the brightness and contrast of the display to
be appropriate for ambient lighting conditions; trade-offs between
character brightness and sharpness may be needed to achieve an
acceptable balance. In many kinds of equipment this is achieved
by providing a control or controls which allow the user to make
adjustments.

Screen adjustability

12   Adjustment mechanisms allow the screen to be tilted or
swivelled to avoid glare and reflections and enable the worker to
maintain a natural and relaxed posture. They may be built into the

screen, form part of the workstation furniture or be provided by separate screen support devices; they should be simple and easy to operate. Screen height adjustment devices, although not essential, may be a useful means of adjusting the screen to the correct height for the worker. (The reference in the Schedule to adjustable tables does not mean these have to be provided).

Glare and reflections

13   Screens are generally manufactured without highly reflective surface finishes but in adverse lighting conditions, reflection and glare may be a problem. Advice on lighting is below (paragraphs 20–24).

Keyboard

14   Keyboard design should allow workers to locate and activate keys quickly, accurately and without discomfort. The choice of keyboard will be dictated by the nature of the task and determined in relation to other elements of the work system. Hand support may be incorporated into the keyboard for support while keying or at rest depending on what the worker finds comfortable, may be provided in the form of a space between the keyboard and front edge of the desk, or may be given by a separate hand/wrist support attached to the work surface.

Work desk or work surface

15   Work surface dimensions may need to be larger than for conventional non-screen office work, to take adequate account of:

(a)   the range of tasks performed (eg screen viewing, keyboard input, use of other input devices, writing on paper etc);

(b)   position and use of hands for each task;

(c)   use and storage of working materials and equipment (documents, telephones etc).

16   Document holders are useful for work with hard copy, particularly for workers who have difficulty in refocussing. They should position working documents at a height, visual plane and, where appropriate, viewing distance similar to those of the screen; be of low reflectance; be stable; and not reduce the readability of source documents.

Work chair

17   The primary requirement here is that the work chair should allow the user to achieve a comfortable position. Seat height

adjustments should accommodate the needs of users for the tasks performed. The Schedule requires the seat to be adjustable in height (ie relative to the ground) and the seat back to be adjustable in height (also relative to the ground) and tilt. Provided the chair design meets these requirements and allows the user to achieve a comfortable posture, it is not necessary for the height or tilt of the seat back to be adjustable independently of the seat. Automatic backrest adjustments are acceptable if they provide adequate back support. General health and safety advice and specifications for seating are given in the HSE publication *Seating at Work* (HS(G)57). A range of publications with detailed advice covering comfort and performance as well as health and safety is included in Annex C.

18   Footrests may be necessary where individual workers are unable to rest their feet flat on the floor (eg where work surfaces cannot be adjusted to the right height in relation to other components of the workstation). Footrests should not be used when they are not necessary as this can result in poor posture.

Environment

Space requirements

19   Prolonged sitting in a static position can be harmful. It is most important that support surfaces for display screen and other equipment and materials used at the workstation should allow adequate clearance for postural changes. This means adequate clearances for thighs, knees, lower legs and feet under the work surface and between furniture components. The height of the work surface should allow a comfortable position for the arms and wrists, if a keyboard is used.

Lighting, reflections and glare

20   Lighting should be appropriate for all the tasks performed at the workstation, eg reading from the screen, keyboard work, reading printed text, writing on paper etc. General lighting – by artificial or natural light, or a combination – should illuminate the entire room to an adequate standard. Any supplementary individual lighting provided to cater for personal needs or a particular task should not adversely affect visual conditions at nearby workstations.

Illuminance

21   High illuminances render screen characters less easy to see but improve the ease of reading documents. Where a high illuminance environment is preferred for this or other reasons, the use of

positive polarity screens (dark characters on a light background) has advantages as these can be used comfortably at higher illuminances than can negative polarity screens.

Reflections and glare

22   Problems which can lead to visual fatigue and stress can arise for example from unshielded bright lights or bright areas in the worker's field of view; from an imbalance between brightly and dimly lit parts of the environment; and from reflections on the screen or other parts of the workstation.

23   Measures to minimise these problems include: shielding, replacing or repositioning sources of light; rearranging or moving work surfaces, documents or all or parts of workstations; modifying the colour or reflectance of walls, ceilings, furnishings etc near the workstation; altering the intensity of vertical to horizontal illuminance; or a combination of these. Anti-glare screen filters should be considered as a last resort if other measures fail to solve the problem.

24   General guidance on minimum lighting standards necessary to ensure health and safety of workplaces is available in the HSE guidance note *Lighting at Work* (HS(G)38). This does not cover ways of using lighting to maximise task performance or enhance the appearance of the workplace, although it does contain a bibliography listing relevant publications in this area. Specific and detailed guidance is given in the CIBSE Lighting Guide 3 *Lighting for visual display terminals*. Full details of these publications are given in Annex C.

Noise

25   Noise from equipment such as printers at display screen workstations should be kept to levels which do not impair concentration or prevent normal conversation (unless the noise is designed to attract attention, eg to warn of a malfunction). Noise can be reduced by replacement, sound-proofing or repositioning of the equipment; sound insulating partitions between noisy equipment and the rest of the workstation are an alternative.

Heat and humidity

26   Electronic equipment can be a source of dry heat which can modify the thermal environment at the workstation. Ventilation and humidity should be maintained at levels which prevent discomfort and problems of sore eyes.

Radiation

27   The Schedule requires radiation with the exception of the visible part of the electromagnetic spectrum (ie visible light) to be reduced to negligible levels from the point of view of the protection of users' health and safety. In fact so little radiation is emitted from current designs of display screen equipment that no special action is necessary to meet this requirement (see also Annex B, paragraphs 8–10).

28   Taking cathode ray tube displays as an example, ionising radiation is emitted only in exceedingly small quantities, so small as to be generally much less than the natural background level to which everyone is exposed. Emissions of ultraviolet, visible and infrared radiation are also very small, and workers will receive much less than the maximum exposures generally recommended by national and international advisory bodies.

29   For radio frequencies, the exposures will also be well below the maximum values generally recommended by national and international advisory bodies for health protection purposes. The levels of electric and magnetic fields are similar to those from common domestic electrical devices. Although much research has been carried out on possible health effects from exposure to electromagnetic radiation, no adverse health effects have been shown to result from the emissions from display screen equipment.

30   Thus it is not necessary, from the standpoint of limiting risk to human health, for employers or workers to take any action to reduce radiation levels or to attempt to measure emissions; in fact the latter is not recommended as meaningful interpretation of the data is very difficult. There is no need for users to be given protective devices such as anti-radiation screens.

Task design and software

Principles of task design

31   Inappropriate task design can be among the causes of stress at work. Stress jeopardises employee motivation, effectiveness and efficiency and in some cases it can lead to significant health problems. The Regulations are only applicable where health and safety rather than productivity is being put at risk; but employers may find it useful to consider both aspects together as task design changes put into effect for productivity reasons may also benefit health, and vice versa.

32   In display screen work, good design of the task can be as important as the correct choice of equipment, furniture and working environment. It is advantageous to:

(a)   design jobs in a way that offers users variety, opportunities to exercise discretion, opportunities for learning, and appropriate feedback, in preference to simple repetitive tasks whenever possible. (For example, the work of a typist can be made less repetitive and stressful if an element of clerical work is added);

(b)   match staffing levels to volumes of work, so that individual users are not subject to stress through being either overworked or underworked;

(c)   allow users to participate in the planning, design and implementation of work tasks whenever possible.

Principles of software ergonomics

33   In most display screen work the software controls both the presentation of information on the screen and the ways in which the worker can manipulate the information. Thus software design can be an important element of task design. Software that is badly designed or inappropriate for the task will impede the efficient completion of the work and in some cases may cause sufficient stress to affect the health of a user. Involving a sample of users in the purchase or design of software can help to avoid problems.

34   Detailed ergonomic standards for software are likely to be developed in future as part of the ISO 9241 standard; for the moment, the Schedule lists a few general principles which employers should take into account. Requirements of the organisation and of display screen workers should be established as the basis for designing, selecting, and modifying software. In many (though not all) applications the main points are:

Suitability for the task

—   Software should enable workers to complete the task efficiently, without presenting unnecessary problems or obstacles.

Ease of use and adaptability

—   Workers should be able to feel that they can master the system and use it effectively following appropriate training;

—   The dialogue between the system and the worker should be appropriate for the worker's ability;

— Where appropriate, software should enable workers to adapt the user interface to suit their ability level and preferences;

— The software should protect workers from the consequences of errors, for example by providing appropriate warnings and information and by enabling 'lost' data to be recovered wherever practicable.

Feedback on system performance

— The system should provide appropriate feedback, which may include error messages; suitable assistance ('help') to workers on request; and messages about changes in the system such as malfunctions or overloading;

— Feedback messages should be presented at the right time and in an appropriate style and format. They should not contain unnecessary information.

Format and pace

— Speed of response to commands and instructions should be appropriate to the task and to workers' abilities;

— Characters, cursor movements and position changes should where possible be shown on the screen as soon as they are input.

Performance monitoring facilities

— Quantitative or qualitative checking facilities built into the software can lead to stress if they have adverse results such as an over-emphasis on output speed;

— It is possible to design monitoring systems that avoid these drawbacks and provide information that is helpful to workers as well as managers. However, in all cases workers should be kept informed about the introduction and operation of such systems.

Appendix C – Possible effects on health from DSE work

The main hazards

1   The introduction of VDUs and other display screen equipment has been associated with a range of symptoms related to the visual system and working posture. These often reflect bodily fatigue. They can readily be prevented by applying ergonomic principles to the design, selection and installation of display screen equipment, the design of the workplace, and the organisation of the task.

Upper limb pains and discomfort

2   A range of conditions of the arm, hand and shoulder areas linked to work activities are now described as work related upper limb disorders. These range from temporary fatigue or soreness in the limb to chronic soft tissue disorders like peritendinitis or carpal tunnel syndrome. Some keyboard operators have suffered occupational cramp.

3   The contribution to the onset of any disorder of individual risk factors (eg keying rates) is not clear. It is likely that a combination of factors are concerned. Prolonged static posture of the back, neck and head are known to cause musculoskeletal problems. Awkward positioning of the hands and wrist (eg as a result of poor working technique or inappropriate work height) are further likely factors. Outbreaks of soft tissue disorders among keyboard workers have often been associated with high workloads combined with tight deadlines. This variety of factors contributing to display screen work risk requires a risk reduction strategy which embraces proper equipment, furniture, training, job design and work planning.

Eye and eyesight effects

4   Medical evidence shows that using display screen equipment is not associated with damage to eyes or eyesight; nor does it make existing defects worse. But some workers may experience **temporary** visual fatigue, leading to a range of symptoms such as impaired visual performance, red or sore eyes and headaches, or the adoption of awkward posture which can cause further discomfort in the limb. These may be caused by:

(a)   staying in the same position and concentrating for a long time;

(b)   poor positioning of the display screen equipment;

(c)   poor legibility of the screen or source documents;

(d)   poor lighting, including glare and reflections;

(e)   a drifting, flickering or jittering image on the screen.

Like other visually demanding tasks, VDU work does not cause eye damage but it may make workers with pre-existing vision defects more aware of them. Such uncorrected defects can make work with a display screen more tiring or stressful than would otherwise be the case.

Fatigue and stress

5   Many symptoms described by display screen workers reflect stresses arising from their task. They may be secondary to upper limb or visual problems but they are more likely to be caused by poor job design or work organisation, particularly lack of sufficient control of the work by the user, under-utilisation of skills, high-speed repetitive working or social isolation. All these have been linked with stress in display screen work, although clearly they are not unique to it; but attributing individual symptoms to particular aspects of a job or workplace can be difficult. The risks of display screen workers experiencing physical fatigue and stress can be minimised, however, by following the principles underlying the Display Screen Equipment Regulations 1992 and guidance, ie by careful design, selection and disposition of display screen equipment; good design of the user's workplace, environment and task; and training, consultation and involvement of the user.

Other concerns

Epilepsy

6   Display screen equipment has not been known to induce epileptic seizures. People suffering from the very rare (1 in 10 000 population) photosensitive epilepsy who react adversely to flickering lights and patterns also find they can safely work with display screens. People with epilepsy who are concerned about display screen work can seek further advice from local offices of the Employment Medical Advisory Service.

Facial dermatitis

7   Some VDU users have reported facial skin complaints such as occasional itching or reddened skin on the face and/or neck. These complaints are relatively rare and the limited evidence available suggests they may be associated with environmental factors, such as low relative humidity or static electricity near the VDU.

Electro magnetic radiation

8   Anxiety about radiation emissions from display screen equipment and possible effects on pregnant women has been widespread. However, there is substantial evidence that these concerns are unfounded. The Health and Safety Executive has consulted the National Radiological Protection Board, which has the statutory function of providing information and advice on all radiation matters to Government Departments, and the advice below summarises scientific understanding.

9   The levels of ionising and non-ionising electromagnetic radiation which are likely to be generated by display screen equipment are well below those set out in international recommendations for limiting risk to human health created by such emissions and the National Radiological Protection Board does not consider such levels to pose a significant risk to health. No special protective measures are therefore needed to protect the health of people from this radiation.

Effects on pregnant women

10   There has been considerable public concern about reports of higher levels of miscarriage and birth defects among some groups of visual display unit (VDU) workers in particular due to electromagnetic radiation. Many scientific studies have been carried out, but taken as a whole their results do not show any link between miscarriages or birth defects and working with VDUs. Research and reviews of the scientific evidence will continue to be undertaken.

11   In the light of the scientific evidence pregnant women do not need to stop work with VDUs. However, to avoid problems caused by stress and anxiety, women who are pregnant or planning children and worried about working with VDUs should be given the opporutnity to discuss their concerns with someone adequately informed of current authoritative scientific information and advice.

3.17   Statutory Requirements for Risk Assessment

Appendix D – HSE version of a DSE assessment form

VDU WORKSTATION CHECKLIST FOR RISK ASSESSMENT AND COMPLYING WITH THE SCHEDULE TO THE REGULATIONS

Workstation number: (if applicable) _____   Date of assessment _____ Any further action needed?:   YES/NO

User: _____   Follow up action completed on: _____

Checklist completed by: _____   Notes for completing: For risk assessments complete columns headed "risk factors" to "action completed" inclusive. Where the answer is 'Yes' in the second column, no further action is necessary.

Assessment checked by: _____

To check equipment complies with the Schedule, answer 'Yes' to questions in the first and last columns.

RISK FACTORS	TICK ANSWER YES NO	HELP	FURTHER ACTION IF NEEDED	ACTION COMPLETED	FURTHER POINTS TO SATISFY WHEN INTRODUCING EQUIPMENT
1 Is the display screen image clear?					
❏ Are the characters readable?		❏ Is the screen clean ?			
		❏ May need supplier's help			
❏ Is the image free of flicker and movement?		❏ Try different screen colour to reduce flicker			
		❏ Still problems? Refer to equipment supplier			
❏ Are the brightness and/or contrast adjustable?		❏ Separate adjustment may not be necessary on latest technology			
❏ Does the screen swivel and tilt?		❏ Swivel and tilt need not be built in.Can you add a tilt mechanism?			
		❏ If work is intensive, and user has problems, may need to replace			

Health and Safety
Executive ✓

RISK FACTORS	TICK ANSWER YES NO	HELP	FURTHER ACTION IF NEEDED	ACTION COMPLETED	FURTHER POINTS TO SATISFY WHEN INTRODUCING EQUIPMENT
❑ Is the screen free from glare and reflections?		❑ Use mirror placed in front of screen to check where reflections are coming from ❑ Try to move the screen, desk or source of reflections ❑ Adjust lighting or window coverings. Check that blinds work (vertical blinds are more effective than horizontal blinds). ❑ If you have tried these suggestions, consider an anti-glare screen filter or seek specialist help			❑ Is the screen surface low reflectance material?
2 Is the keyboard comfortable?					
❑ Is the keyboard tiltable?		❑ Tilt need not be built in			
❑ Can you find a comfortable keying position?		❑ Is the user keying properly? ○ hands shouldn't be bent up at the wrist ○ is user applying a soft touch on the keys? ○ is the user over-stretching the fingers? ❑ Is the keyboard separate from the screen? ❑ Does the keyboard need repositioning? If not separate from the screen, may need replacing			
❑ Is there enough space to rest hands in front of the keyboard?		❑ Can VDU monitor be pushed further back? (see 3 below)			
❑ Is the keyboard glare free?		❑ Seek supplier's help			
❑ Are the characters on the keys easily readable?		❑ Keyboard may need cleaning, modifying or replacing			

3.17   Statutory Requirements for Risk Assessment

RISK FACTORS	TICK ANSWER YES NO	HELP	FURTHER ACTION IF NEEDED	ACTION COMPLETED	FURTHER POINTS TO SATISFY WHEN INTRODUCING EQUIPMENT
3 Does the furniture 'fit' the work and the user?					
❑ Is the work surface large enough for documents, monitor, keyboard, etc?		❑ Can printer/files etc go elsewhere to make more room? ❑ Is the user making repeated or awkward stretching movements? ❑ Can you rearrange equipment, paper or work to avoid discomfort? ❑ May need to provide more space or resite sockets			❑ Is it large enough to take all of the necessary equipment, keyboard etc in a variety of layouts?
❑ Is the surface free of glare reflections?		❑ Consider mats or blotters for larger areas ❑ Contact the supplier			❑ Does the workstation furniture have a low reflectance surface?

❑ Is the chair stable?
 	
❑ Do the adjustment mechanisms work?
 	
❑ Are you comfortable?
		❑ It may need repair or replacing in 1996 if it does not adjust. If the user is uncomfortable it may need replacing now
		
		❑ Is the user sitting properly? Try adjusting chair
		
		  ○ are arms horizontal and eyes at roughly the same height as the top of the VDU casing?
		  ○ are feet flat on the floor?
		  ○ too much pressure on backs of legs and knees may mean a foot rest is needed
		  ○ is the small of the back supported by the chair?
		  ○ is the back straight, but supported and shoulders relaxed, or is user leaning forward?
		  ○ are arms of chair (if any) preventing user getting close enough to key comfortably?
		
		❑ Are there obstructions under the desk that need to be moved?
					❑ Does it swivel?
					
					❑ Does the seat height adjust?
					
					❑ Does the seat back adjust in height and tilt?

RISK FACTORS	TICK ANSWER YES NO	HELP	FURTHER ACTION IF NEEDED	ACTION COMPLETED	FURTHER POINTS TO SATISFY WHEN INTRODUCING EQUIPMENT
4 Is the environment around the workstation risk-free?					
❑ Is there enough room to change position and vary movement?		❑ User needs space to fidget ❑ Will reorganising office layout help? ❑ Check for obstructions			❑ Is there adequate room for the workstation?
❑ Are the levels of light, heat and noise comfortable?		❑ Light could be too bright, or not bright enough to comfortably read by. Consider shading or repositioning light sources or consider more lighting, eg table light ❑ Can you distance user from sources of noise or heat (eg printer)? If not, consider sound-proofing or increase ventilation			❑ Is it suitable lighting for VDU work? ❑ Is it being sited in the best place? ❑ Is equipment quiet? ❑ What about when a lot is in one area? ❑ Will more equipment significantly raise the temperature?
❑ Does the air feel comfortable?		❑ Equipment may dry the air: circulation of fresh air where possible, and plants may help ❑ Consider a humidifier if discomfort severe			❑ How will reasonable humidity be achieved?
5 Is the software user-friendly?					
❑ Can you comfortably use the software?		❑ Has the user had enough training?			❑ Is the software suitable for the task? ❑ Can it be easily used with appropriate training? ❑ Does it give feedback, eg adequate help messages?
❑ Has this checklist covered all of the comfort problems you might have working with your VDU?					

3.17   Statutory Requirements for Risk Assessment

Appendix E – Example of a typical DSE assessment form

DISPLAY SCREEN EQUIPMENT - WORKSTATION SELF-ASSESSMENT FORM

USER NAME	
WORKSTATION LOCATION	
WORK STATION NO.	
DATE ASSESSMENT UNDERTAKEN	

Please complete this form by putting ticks in the **YES** or **NO** box alongside each question. Relate your answers to your use of your workstation.

	RISK FACTORS	YES	NO	HELP
1	IS THE DISPLAY SCREEN IMAGE CLEAR?			
1.1	Are the characters readable?			*Is the screen clean?*
1.2	Is the image free of flicker and movement?			*Try different screen colour to reduce flicker. Still problems, refer to ITU*
1.3	Are the brightness and/or contrast adjustable?			
1.4	Does the screen swivel and tilt?			
1.5	Is the screen free from glare and reflections?			*Try to move screen, desk or source of reflections Adjust lighting or window coverings. Check that blinds work. If these suggestions have been tried consider an anti-glare screen filter.*
2	IS THE KEYBOARD COMFORTABLE?			
2.1	Is the keyboard tiltable?			
2.2	Can you find a comfortable keying position?			*Is the user keying properly?-* • *hands should be bent* • *is user applying a soft touch on keys?* • *is the user over-stretching fingers?* *Does the keyboard need repositioning?*
2.3	Are you able to use the mouse comfortably?			*Is there space beside the keyboard to use mouse? Do you have a mouse mat?*

	RISK FACTORS	YES	NO	HELP
2.4	Is there enough space to rest hands in front of keyboard?			*Can the monitor be pushed further back?*
2.5	Is the keyboard free of glare?			
2.6	Are the characters on the keys easily readable?			*Keyboard may need cleaning, modifying or replacing.*
3	**DOES THE FURNITURE 'FIT' THE WORK AND THE USER?**			
3.1	Is the work surface large enough for documents, monitor, keyboard etc?			*Can printer or files etc go elsewhere to make more room? Is the user making repeated and awkward stretching movements? Can you rearrange equipment, paper or work to avoid discomfort? May need to provide more space or resite sockets?*
3.2	Is the surface free of glare reflections?			*Consider mats or blotters for larger areas.*
3.3	Is the chair stable?			*It may need repair or replacing if it does not adjust.*
3.4	Do the adjustment mechanisms work?			*If the user is uncomfortable it may need replacing now.*
3.5	Are you comfortable?			*Is the user sitting properly* • *are arms horizontal and eyes roughly the same height as the top of the VDU casing?* • *Are feet flat on the floor?* • *Too much pressure on the backs of legs and knees may mean a foot rest in needed* • *Is the small of the back supported by the chair?* • *Is the back straight, but supported and shoulders relaxed or is user leaning forward?* • *are arms of chair (if any) preventing user getting close enough to key comfortably?* *Are there any obstructions under the desk that need to be moved?*

3.17 Statutory Requirements for Risk Assessment

	RISK FACTORS	YES	NO	HELP
4	**IS THE ENVIRONMENT AROUND THE WORKSTATION RISK FREE?**			
4.1	Is there enough room to change position and vary movement?			*User needs space to fidget* *Will reorganising office layout help?* *Check for obstructions*
4.2	Are there comfortable levels of - Heat? Light? Noise?			*Light could be too bright, or not bright enough to comfortably read by. Consider shading or repositioning light sources. Can you distance user from sources or noise or heat?*
4.3	Does the air feel comfortable?			*Equipment may dry the air: circulation of fresh air where possible and plants may help. Consider a humidifier if discomfort is severe.*
5	**IS THE SOFTWARE USER-FRIENDLY?**			
5.1	Can you comfortably use the software?			*Has the user had enough training?*
	Has this checklist covered all of the comfort problems you might have working with your VDU?			
6	**INFORMATION AND TRAINING?**			
6.1	Have you been given advice on when to take rest breaks?			
6.2	Have you been properly instructed on how to adjust your - Chair? Screen? Keyboard?			
6.3	Have you been informed about your rights to have an eye vision test?			

Appendix F – Form recording action to be taken in respect to negative responses by users during workstation assessment

Ticks in the 'NO' column indicate potential risks to the "User" using this particular workstation. These risks should be listed below and an assessment of necessary remedial action made. It is also important to record who is responsible for implementing that action.

Question No	RISK	ACTION TO BE TAKEN

ASSESSORS NAME	ACTION TAKEN BY
....	NAME ....
DATE	DATE ....

3.17 Statutory Requirements for Risk Assessment

Appendix G – DSE Summary sheet

SER #	USER NAME	Wk Station Loc	DISPLAY SCREEN								KEYBOARD				FURNITURE										WORKING ENVIRONMENT						SOFTWARE	REQUIREMENTS	COMMENTS
			1.0	1.1	1.2	1.3	1.4	1.5	2.0	2.1	2.2	2.3	2.4	2.5	2.6	3.0	3.1	3.2	3.3	3.4	3.5	4.0	4.1	4.2	4.3	5.0	5.1		
	B/FORWARD																												
	C/FORWARD																												

Requirements column headings: A/G FILTER, L/E C H A R R, F/O L E A R, O V U S T, O O T L E A D, M T H E T R, E E S E, H A L, T D R

Notes on completion.

1. Enter a cross only for those questions where the user answers "No" to any question
2. If a user makes a written comment insert word "Yes" in comments column
3. The "Requirements" columns should be ticked if the user requests any of the items listed. These are anti-glare filter, chair, desk leveller, footrest, mouse aid or pad. "other" includes document holders

NB: This summary sheet matches the questions in the assessment forms appearing as appendices E and F

Appendix H – Basic principles of safe manual handling

173   A good handling technique is no substitute for other risk reduction steps such as improvements to the task, load or working environment. In addition, moving the load by rocking, pivoting, rolling or sliding is preferable to lifting it in situations where scope for risk reduction is limited. However, good handling technique forms a very valuable adjunct to other risk control measures. It requires both training and practice. The training should be carried out in conditions that are as realistic as possible, emphasising its relevance to everyday handling operations.

174   There is no single correct way to lift and many different approaches are put forward. Each has merits and advantages in particular situations or individual circumstances. The content of training in good handling technique, therefore, should be tailored to the particular handling operations likely to be undertaken. It should begin with relatively simple examples and progress to more specialised handling operations as appropriate. The following list illustrates some important points, using a basic lifting operation by way of example:

(a)   **Stop and think.** Plan the lift. Where is the load going to be placed? Use appropriate handling aids if possible. Do you need help with the load? Remove obstructions such as discarded wrapping materials. For a long lift – such as floor to shoulder height – consider resting the load mid-way on a table or bench to change grip.

(b)   **Place the feet.** Have the feet apart, giving a balanced and stable base for lifting (tight skirts and unsuitable footwear make this difficult). Have the leading leg as far forward as is comfortable.

(c)   **Adopt a good posture.** Bend the knees so that the hands when grasping the load are as nearly level with the waist as possible. But do not kneel or overflex the knees. Keep the back straight, maintaining its natural curve (tucking in the chin while gripping the load helps). Lean forward a little over the load if necessary to get a good grip. Keep shoulders level and facing in the same direction as the hips.

(d) **Get a firm grip.** Try to keep the arms within the boundary formed by the legs. The optimum position and nature of the grip depends on the circumstances and individual preference, but it must be secure. A hook grip is less fatiguing than keeping the fingers straight. If it is necessary to vary the grip as the lift proceeds, do this as smoothly as possible.

(e) **Don't jerk.** Carry out the lifting movement smoothly, raising the chin as the lift begins, keeping control of the load.

(f) **Move the feet.** Don't twist the trunk when turning to the side.

(g) **Keep close to the load.** Keep the load close to the trunk for as long as possible. Keep the heaviest side of the load next to the trunk. If a close approach to the load is not possible try sliding it towards you before attempting to lift it.

(h) **Put down,** *then* adjust. If precise positioning of the load is necessary, put it down first, then slide it into the desired position.

Appendix I – Manual handling risk assessment – detailed assessment guidelines filter

Introduction

1   The Manual Handling Regulations set no specific requirements such as weight limits. Instead, they focus on the needs of the
individual and set out a hierarchy of measures for safety during
manual handling operations:

(a)   avoid hazardous manual handling operations so far as is
reasonably practicable;

(b)   make a suitable and sufficient assessment of any hazardous
manual handling operations that cannot be avoided; and

(c)   reduce the risk of injury from those operations so far as is
reasonably practicable.

Risk assessment filter

2   Where manual handling operations cannot be avoided,
employers have a duty to make a suitable and sufficient assessment
of the risks to health. This assessment must take into account the
range of relevant factors listed in Schedule 1 to the Regulations. A
detailed assessment of every manual handling operation, however,
could be a major undertaking and might involve wasted effort.
Many handling operations, for example lifting a tea cup, will
involve negligible handling risk. To help identify situations where
a more detailed risk assessment is necessary, HSE has developed a
filter to screen out straightforward cases.

3   The filter is based on a set of numerical guidelines developed
from data in published scientific literature and on practical experience of assessing risks from manual handling. They are pragmatic,
tried and tested; they are not based on any precise scientific
formulae. The intention is to set out an approximate boundary
within which the load is unlikely to create a risk of injury sufficient
to warrant a detailed assessment.

4   The application of the guidelines will provide a reasonable
level of protection to around 95% of working men and women.
However, the guidelines should not be regarded as safe weight
limits for lifting. There is no threshold below which manual
handling operations may be regarded as 'safe'. Even operations
lying within the boundary mapped out by the guidelines should be
avoided or made less demanding wherever it is reasonably practicable to do so.

5   It is important to remember that the purpose of the guidelines is to avoid wasted time and effort. The use of the filter will only be worthwhile, therefore, where the relevance of the guideline figures can be determined quickly, say within 10 minutes. If it is not clear from the outset that this can be done, it is better to opt immediately for the more detailed risk assessment.

Guidelines for lifting and lowering

6   The guidelines for lifting and lowering operations assume that the load is easy to grasp with both hands and that the operation takes place in reasonable working conditions with the handler in a stable body position. They take into consideration the vertical and horizontal position of the hands as they move the load during the handling operation, as well as the height and reach of the individual handler. For example if a load is held at arm's length or the hands pass above shoulder height, the capability to lift or lower is reduced significantly.

7   The basic guideline figures for identifying when manual lifting and lowering operations may not need a detailed assessment are set out below. If the handler's hands enter more than one of the box zones during the operation, the smallest weight figures apply. It is important to remember, however, that the transition from one box zone to another is not abrupt; an intermediate figure may be chosen where the handler's hands are close to a boundary. Where lifting or lowering with the hands beyond the box zones is unavoidable, a more detailed assessment should always be made.

Lifting and lowering

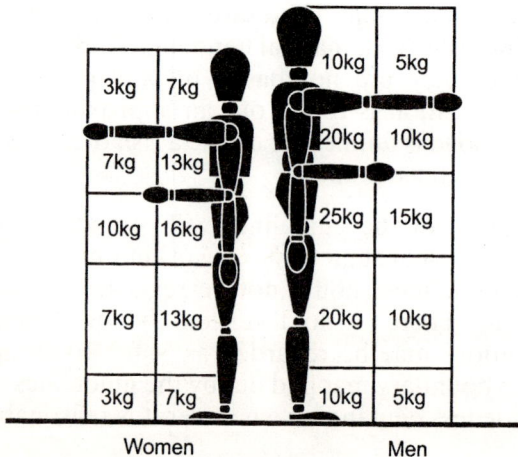

Women   Men

68

8   These basic guideline figures for lifting and lowering are for relatively infrequent operations – up to approximately 30 operations per hour. The guideline figures will have to be reduced if the operation is repeated more often. As a rough guide, the figures should be reduced by 30% where the operation is repeated once or twice per minute, by 50% where the operation is repeated around five to eight times per minute and by 80% where the operation is repeated more than about 12 times per minute.

9   Even if the above conditions are satisfied, a more detailed risk assessment should be made where:

(a)   the worker does not control the pace of work;

(b)   pauses for rest are inadequate or there is no change of activity which provides an opportunity to use different muscles;

(c)   the handler must support the load for any length of time.

Guidelines for carrying

10   Similar guideline figures apply to carrying operations where the load is held against the body and is carried no further than about 10 m without resting. If the load is carried over a longer distance without resting or the hands are below knuckle height then a more detailed risk assessment should be made.

11   Where the load can be carried securely on the shoulder without first having to be lifted (as for example when unloading sacks from a lorry) the guideline figures can be applied to carrying distances in excess of 10 m.

Guidelines for pushing and pulling

12   For pushing and pulling operations (whether the load is slid, rolled or supported on wheels) the guideline figures assume the force is applied with the hands between knuckle and shoulder height. The guideline figure for starting or stopping the load is a force of about 25 kg (ie about 250 Newtons) for men and about 16 kg (ie about 160 Newtons) for women. The guideline figure for keeping the load in motion is a force of about 10 kg (ie about 100 Newtons) for men and about 7 kg (ie about 70 Newtons) for women.

13   There is no specific limit to the distance over which the load is pushed or pulled provided there are adequate opportunities for rest or recovery.

Handling while seated

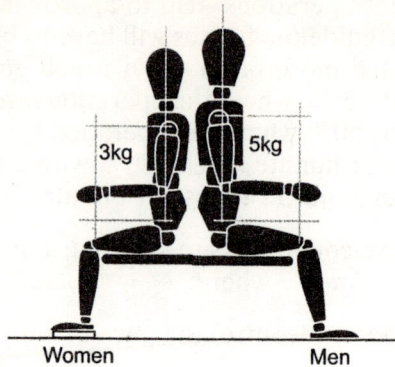

Women   Men

Guidelines for handling while seated

14   The basic guideline figure for handling operations carried out while seated, shown above, is 5 kg for men and 3 kg for women. These guidelines only apply when the hands are within the box zone indicated. If handling beyond the box zone is unavoidable, a more detailed assessment should be made.

Other considerations: Twisting

15   In many cases, manual handling operations will involve some twisting (see below) and this will increase the risk of injury. Where

Assessing twist

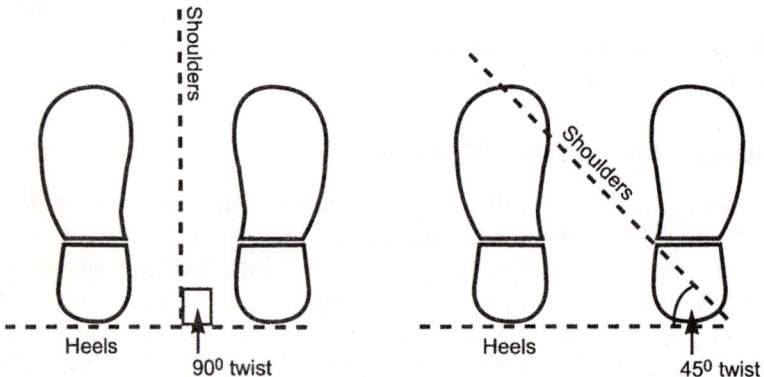

the handling task involves twisting and turning, therefore, a detailed risk assessment should normally be made. However, if the operation is relatively infrequent (see paragraph 8 of this Appendix) and there are no other posture problems then the filter can be used. In such cases, the basic guideline figures shown above should be reduced if the handler twists to the side during the operation.

As a rough guide, the figures should be reduced by about 10% where the handler twists through 45° and by about 20% where the handler twists through 90°.

Remember: The use of these guidelines does not affect the employer's duty to avoid or reduce risk of injury where this is reasonably practicable. The guideline figures, therefore, should not be regarded as weight limits for safe lifting. They are an aid to highlight where detailed risk assessments are most needed. Where doubt remains, a more detailed risk assessment should always be made. Even for a minority of fit, well-trained individuals working under favourable conditions, operations which exceed the guideline figures by more than a factor of about two may represent a serious risk of injury. Such operations should come under very close scrutiny.

Appendix J – Assessment checklist example

1   A suitable and sufficient risk assessment is required when hazardous manual handling is unavoidable. The assessment should identify where the risk lies and suggest an appropriate range of ideas for reducing the potential for injury. A checklist can help with this process by ensuring a systematic examination of all the potential risk elements.

2   An example of a basic checklist is provided on pages 48–49. Its use will help to highlight the overall level of risk involved and identify how the job may be modified to reduce the risk of injury and make it easier to do. It will also be useful in helping to prioritise the remedial actions needed. The checklist may be copied freely or may be used to help design your own assessment checklist.

3   The following notes are intended to assist in completing the checklist.

(a)   **Section A: *Describe*** the job. There is space available for a diagram to be drawn to summarise the job in a picture, as well as for a written description.

(b)   **Section B: *Tick*** the level of risk you believe to be associated with each of the items on the list. Space is provided for noting the precise nature of the problem and for suggestions about the remedial action that may be taken. It may also be useful to write down the names of the relevant people or groups in your organisation who you will wish to consult about implementing the remedial steps, for example managers, workforce trainers, maintenance personnel or engineers.
Some tasks may involve more than one operator, each with a different level of risk, depending on the exact nature of their duties. If you wish to use the same checklist for all of the operators involved, you can allocate a number (or other identifying mark) to each and use that against each tick (eg $\checkmark^1$; $\checkmark^{1/2}$; $\checkmark^{1/2/3}$; etc) or comment on the checklist form that relates to each particular operator.

(c)   **Section C: *Decide*** whether the overall risk of injury is low, medium or high. This section will help to prioritise remedial action if you have a large number of risk assessments to carry out.

(d)   **Section D: *Summarise*** the remedial steps that should be taken, in order of priority. You may also wish to write in (**I**), (**M**) or (**L**) alongside each entry to denote whether the action can be taken (**I**)**mmediately** or is a more (**M**)**edium-term** or

(L)ong-term objective. The assessor's name and the date by which the agreed actions should be carried out should be recorded. It may also be useful to enter the target date for reassessment if this is appropriate.

4   When all the manual handling tasks have been assessed, the completed checklists can be compared to help prioritise the most urgent actions. However, there are likely to be several ways to reduce the risks identified and some will be more effective than others. Action on those that can be implemented easily and quickly should not be delayed simply because they may be less effective than others.

5   A check should be carried out at a later date to ensure that the remedial action to remove or reduce the risk of injury has been effective.

6   A worked example of a risk assessment made using the checklist is given on pages 76–77 to show how the checklist might be used in practice.

7   The purpose of the checklist is to help bring out a range of ideas on how the risks identified can be avoided or reduced by making modifications to the load, the task, and the working environment. There are a number of people who may be able to help with suggestions, for example safety representatives, the quality management team within the organisation, and relevant trade associations. There is also a great deal of published information about risk reduction methods. *Solutions you can handle* and *A pain in your workplace*, both published by HSE, give examples that are relevant to situations across many sectors of industry. Trade journals, too, often contain information about products that can be used to help reduce the risk of injury from the manual handling of loads.

3.17   Statutory Requirements for Risk Assessment

Manual Handling of Loads: Assessment checklist

Section A - Preliminary: *Circle as appropriate

Job description: Factors beyond the limits of the guidelines?	Is an assessment needed? (ie is there a potential risk for injury, and are the factors beyond the limits of the guidelines?) Yes/No*

If 'Yes' continue. If 'No' the assessment need go no further.

Operations covered by this assessment (detailed description): Locations: Personnel involved: Date of assessment:	Diagrams (other information):

Section B - See over for detailed analysis

Section C - Overall assessment of the risk of injury?   Low/ Med/ High*

Section D - Remedial action to be taken:

Remedial steps that should be taken, in order of priority:
1
2
3
4
5
6
7
8
Date by which action should be taken:
Date for reassessment:
Assessor's name: Signature:

TAKE ACTION ... AND CHECK THAT IT HAS THE DESIRED EFFECT

Section B - More detailed assessment, where necessary:

Questions to consider:	If yes, tick appropriate level of risk			Problems occurring from the task (Make rough notes in this column in preparation for the possible remedial action to be taken)	Possible remedial action (Possible changes to be made to system/task, load, workplace/space, environment. Communication that is needed)
	Low	Med	High		
The tasks - do they involve: • holding loads away from trunk? • twisting? • stooping? • reaching upwards? • large vertical movement? • long carrying distances? • strenuous pushing or pulling? • unpredictable movement of loads? • repetitive handling? • insufficient rest or recovery? • a work rate imposed by a process?					
The loads - are they: • heavy? • bulky/unwieldy? • difficult to grasp? • unstable/unpredictable? • intrinsically harmful (eg sharp/hot)?					
The working environment - are there: • constraints on posture? • poor floors? • variations in levels? • hot/cold/humid conditions? • strong air movements? • poor lighting conditions?					
Individual capability - does the job: • require unusual capability? • hazard those with a health problem? • hazard those who are pregnant? • call for special information/training?					
Other factors: Is movement or posture hindered by clothing or personal protective equipment?	Yes/No				

3.17   Statutory Requirements for Risk Assessment

Manual Handling of Loads : Assessment checklist
Worked example

Section A - Preliminary: *circle as appropriate

Job description: **Pallet loading : boxes containing coiled wire**	Is an assessment needed? (ie is there a potential risk for injury, and are the factors beyond the limits of the guidelines?) (Yes)/No*

If 'Yes' continue. If 'No' the assessment need go no further.

Operations covered by this assessment (detailed description): **Operator lifts box, with hook grip, from conveyor, which is 20 inches above the ground, turns, walks 3 metres and lowers box onto a pallet on the ground. Boxes are piled six high on pallet.** Locations: **Wire factory only** Personnel involved: **One operator** Date of assessment: **xx June 19xx**	Diagrams (other information): a) **Worker;** b) **Conveyor;** c) **48 kg boxes of wire;** d) **Pallet.** Arrows show direction of conveyor belt and worker movements between conveyor and pallet

Section B - See over for detailed analysis

Section C - Overall assessment of the risk of injury?   Low/ Med/ (High)

Section D - Remedial action to be taken:

Remedial steps that should be taken, in order of priority: 1 **Review product design to reduce weight of load and improve grip.** 2 **Review process in light of changes agreed in (1), particularly on customer requirements and transportation.** 3 **Seek funding for magnetic lifting aid to help with transfer from conveyor to pallet.** 4 **Seek funding for pallet rotating/height adjustment equipment.** 5 **Operator to attend manual handling training.** 6 **Raise conveyor height by 15 inches.** 7 **Ensure full pallets are removed by pallet truck promptly.** 8 **Operations manager to ensure no rushing on this job.**
Date by which action should be taken: **xx December 19xx**
Date for reassessment: **xx December 20xx**
Assessor's name: **A N Onymous**   Signature: **A N Onymous**

Section B - More detailed assessment, where necessary:

Questions to consider:	If yes, tick appropriate level of risk			Problems occurring from the task (Make rough notes in this column in preparation for the possible remedial action to be taken)	Possible remedial action (Possible changes to be made to system/task, load, workplace/space, environment. Communication that is needed)
	Low	Med	High		
The tasks - do they involve:					
• holding loads away from trunk?	✓			1 Twisting when picking up the box	Remind operator of need to move feet (I).
• twisting?	✓	✓			
• stooping?	✓		✓	2 Stooping when placing box on pallet and stooping when picking box up from the conveyor	Adjust pallet height - Review availability of rotating, height adjusting equipment (I) and raise height of conveyor (M).
• reaching upwards?	✓				
• large vertical movement?	✓			3 Sometimes extended reaching when placing boxes on pallet.	Provide better information and instruction (I).
• long carrying distances?	✓				Review mechanical handling equipment to eliminate manual lifting (I).
• strenuous pushing or pulling?	✓				
• unpredictable movement of loads?	✓				
• repetitive handling?	✓				
• insufficient rest or recovery?					
• a workrate imposed by a process?					
The loads - are they:					
• heavy?	✓		✓	4 Load too heavy. Is the weight of the load a problem for customers too?	Review product and customer needs with a view to improving product design (L).
• bulky/unwieldy?	✓				
• difficult to grasp?	✓	✓		5 Smooth cardboard boxes are difficult to grasp.	Provide boxes with hand grips (M).
• unstable/unpredictable?	✓				
• intrinsically harmful (eg sharp/hot)?					
The working environment - are there:					
• constraints on posture?	✓	✓		6 Bad postures encouraged by obstructions when full pallets are not removed.	Introduce system to ensure full pallets removed promptly - Speak to Operations Manager *(I)*.
• poor floors?	✓				
• variations in levels?	✓				
• hot/cold/humid conditions?	✓				
• strong air movements?	✓				
• poor lighting conditions?					
Individual capability - does the job:					
• require unusual capability?			✓	7 Operator has no history of back pain problems but clear signs of sweating and straining.	Consider job enlargement to introduce variety and allow for recovery time (M).
• hazard those with a health problem?			✓		Monitor to ensure no rushing (I).
• hazard those who are pregnant?			✓		Speak to trainer about manual handling course (I).
• call for special information/training?		✓			
Other factors:					
Is movement or posture hindered by clothing or personal protective equipment?	Yes/No				

4 Risk Assessment — Preparation

Introduction and purpose

4.1   Preparation and planning are key to the success of any workplace activity. When there is failure to plan and prepare as a prelude to risk assessment, the outcome could be serious, not only in jeopardising the health and safety of employees or others and potentially damaging the image of the company, but in exposing the business or organisation to the possibility of criminal prosecution and litigation.

The purpose of this chapter is to consider organisational approaches to the risk assessment process and the various aids and inputs available to assist those responsible for developing the assessment; in short to prepare and plan for risk assessment.

Layout of this chapter

4.2   The chapter is in two parts, Part I considers organisational aspects of preparation and Part II aids and inputs.

Time and space

4.3   As the requirement to develop risk assessments has existed since 1 January 1993, most organisations will have already taken some action to comply. In these cases, this handbook will serve either as a reminder and checklist or to generate ideas for implementation when reviewing an existing assessment, which of course should happen at regular intervals.

For those who have not formally addressed the statutory requirement of *regulation 3* of the *Management of Health and Safety at Work Regulations 1992*, the handbook will assist them to get started without further delay.

Part I — Organisation for risk assessment

Who will be involved?

4.4   The short answer is that everyone should be involved to some degree. It was postulated in Chapter 1 that to develop risk assessments in isolation of those who actually do the work and therefore take the risks, is wrong for a number of reasons:

- Risk assessors would be deprived of vital input and information essential to the process.

- Such exclusion would be a breach of the statutory requirement for employers to consult employees or their representatives in respect to health and safety matters.

- The morale of workers, particularly those engaged in inherently dangerous activities, would suffer if they learned that a company risk assessment had been carried in respect to their work tasks without considering their views.

Benefits of company-wide involvement

4.5   Company or organisation wide involvement in risk considerations brings about another, perhaps greater benefit than those described above – that of engendering appreciation and understanding of the fact that risk assessment is and will remain central to the workplace and working life.

It should be axiomatic for employees to pose the question 'What effect will this have on our current risk assessment?' if the activity, process or area in which they work is changed or altered in any way; risk assessment must not be seen as a passing phase, rather a routine aspect of work.

This objective will not be achieved if risk assessment is viewed by workers as mysterious and beyond their comprehension, something that only management deal with and which usually results in some new rules for them to comply with.

Health and Safety Representatives

4.6   If everyone at work has the right to express views about risks, there must be a framework and organisation within which to express these views. Now that there is universal suffrage in respect to health and safety matters created by the *Safety Representatives and Safety Committees Regulations 1977* and the *Health and Safety (Consultation with Employees) Regulations 1996* respectively, it may be appropriate to channel employee input to the risk assessment process through the representatives appointed in compliance with these regulations.

Safety representatives have an important role to play in respect to risk assessment, and in many organisations they will be the interface between workers and management in gathering, filtering and consolidating the views of those they represent.

Whether or not safety representatives are invited to assemble input regarding risks from those that they represent, they – or at least some of them – should be part of the company risk assessment organisation, the composition of which is discussed in paragraphs 4.10–4.12. However, there might be circumstance where safety representatives could feel uncomfortable or not sufficiently experienced or trained to analyse and assess postulations on risk made by workers. For example, a company might have safety representatives who look after the interests of a number of small groups of employees, where each constituent group work on discrete or complex processes, the full details of which are not disclosed to others.

The final decision on the method of consolidating input from individuals or groups of employees must rest with employers in discussion with employee representatives. Given the purpose and objectives of risk assessment, a mutually acceptable approach ought not to be difficult to achieve.

The role of line managers

4.7   There is one other key factor having a bearing upon the method adopted for risk information collection. This is the role, responsibility and position of line management. In the final analysis, all line managers, and first-level managers in particular, are answerable for health and safety insofar as their department or operation are concerned.

Although considerable advances in organisational theory have been made since the passing of the *Health and Safety at Work etc. Act 1974*, there are still a number of businesses whose managers mistakenly believe that their responsibility for health and safety is either non-existent or is a tenuous one, because they have access to the support of safety officers, safety advisers and other related specialists.

It is therefore important that all managers clearly understand that they have unequivocal responsibility for all health and safety matters within their sphere of control, and that this responsibility includes and embraces risk related matters. There is therefore no question of managers taking a back seat while the safety representatives for their areas are dealing with risk assessment consolidation. The following table considers options for ensuring appropriate involvement in the risk process by managers and safety representatives.

Table 1 — Options for assembling risk information/input from employees

Assembling risk information	Reviewing the information
Safety representative	First-level manager
Safety representative together with first-level manager	No local review — company risk assessment group review findings
First-level manager	Dept/area safety representative

Notes: Where appropriate, the term 'First level manager' includes the manager and supervisors reporting to him/her.

The purpose and role of the company risk assessment group (RAG) are discussed in paragraphs 4.10–4.12.

Some organisations opt to regard the local, i.e. first-level risk assessments as the final version, so that the company risk assessment comprises a collection of individual department assessments, plus the 'general risks' which are explained below.

Central (company) review of risk assessments

4.8   There will invariably be some risks which are applicable to all the workforce, irrespective of the nature of their work, an example being fire related risks. These are the 'common risks'.

In all cases, however, it will be necessary to review all the individual department/process risk assessments centrally, to ensure that there are no major variances in evaluation where the risk profiles are similar or even identical.

An example would be where a number of departments did precisely the same work, yet some of the department risk assessments produced markedly different results to others. Such inconsistency could be incriminating, for example in the event of a serious accident in a department whose assessment had attached less importance to the risk which precipitated the accident than those of the other departments doing the same or similar work.

Generic risk assessments

4.9   It is important to ensure a degree of consistency when assessing risks in respect to work which is similar if not the same in nature. This has given rise to what have been termed 'generic risk assessments', which are used where the same work processes are carried out by different departments or in different locations of the same organisation.

There is a place for the generic risk assessment, providing that when it is used, there is careful evaluation to ensure that there are no local factors or conditions which compromise the efficacy of the generic assessment. One method of ensuring that local review takes place before a generic assessment is adopted is to require the person 'signing-off' the assessment to certify that nothing about the circumstances of the work or operation which is subject to the generic risk assessment in question affects the validity of the generic assessment.

Subject to this important reservation, which must always be borne in mind, generic risk assessments can provide real benefits. These include saving in time, consistency of approach, a broader overview of the subject, increased opportunities for innovation in combating and controlling the risk, etc.

The Risk Assessment Group (RAG)

4.10 Given the key role of risk assessment in improving and maintaining the highest standards of health and safety at work, the fact that risk assessment is an ongoing activity and not least that there is a statutory requirement to develop and maintain 'suitable and sufficient' risk assessments, it is clear that an appropriate organisation needs to exist within every firm in order to manage and give overall direction in respect to risk assessment.

This organisation must have authority and status. It should report to an executive of board level, and be required to report to the board at least annually.

Composition, roles and responsibilities of the RAG

Overall Responsibility

4.11 To ensure compliance with the risk assessment requirements of *regulation 3* of the *Management of Health and Safety at Work Regulations 1992* and all other applicable regulations requiring the assessment of risks.

Specific responsibilities – see paragraph 4.14.

Composition

4.12 The composition of a typical Risk Assessment Group follows. Precise numbers will vary depending upon the size of the organisation, nature of the business and general risk profile.

Chairman — An executive assigned responsibility for the company risk assessment programme.

Members — A manager from each function, for example R&D, marketing, manufacturing, administration etc. with an equal number of safety representatives.

Specialists

4.13 The Company Safety Adviser/s appointed *per regulation 6* of *MHSWR*, company doctor, occupational health nurse, and other specialists where applicable.

Table 2 — Typical responsibilities of a company Risk Assessment Group

> - Provide advice on all aspects of risk assessment
>
> - Ensure that a 'suitable and sufficient' risk assessment exists for all company operations
>
> - Consider and approve department/operation risk assessments
>
> - Consider and approve all proposed generic risk assessments
>
> - Ensure regular communication of risk assessment matters across the company
>
> - Provide assistance during the initial (local) assessment of risks
>
> - Prepare reports on progress for the company board
>
> - Act as the reference point for published guidance and impending legislation affecting or likely to affect the way that risks are managed within the company
>
> - Publish details of risk assessment considerations and methodologies to be applied to risk evaluation within the company.

Specific responsibilities

4.14 The list of responsibilities in Table 2 is not exhaustive nor will it be necessary in every case for the RAG to discharge all the duties shown. The final list will be a function of the organisational arrangements for carrying out risk assessment in the company or organisation. However it is important to ensure that all of the duties listed are assigned somewhere within the company.

4.15   Risk Assessment — Preparation

Risk Assessment Group workload

4.15   The wide ranging remit of the RAG demonstrates its pivotal role in ensuring that risk assessment is properly managed and implemented. Its composition and size should be sufficient to create any sub-committees necessary to focus on particular topics/issues and provide resources to assist individual departments when needed.

The work of the RAG should not occupy its members full-time, although the volume of work will be heavy at the commencement of the risk assessment programme. Once the programme is well established, plenary meetings at monthly intervals should suffice, with most work being carried out by sub-committees.

Part II — Aids and inputs to the risk assessment process

4.16   Chapter 5 describes methodologies for carrying out risk assessments. However, before any assessment work commences, those who will be doing the work must be cognisant of a number of factors having a bearing upon the process. These factors are considered.

Standards

(i) Legal standards

4.17   When considering ways to eliminate or reduce risks, there are some standards to guide assessors, the most important of which are statutory requirements. If there is a legal standard or requirement, this has to be complied with. There is not and cannot be a regulation covering every conceivable workplace risk; nonetheless there are a considerable number of regulations in existence.

The list which follows is not exhaustive, but serves to illustrate the scope and diversity of legislation aimed at protecting those involved in particular work activities:

- Asbestos – *Control of Asbestos at Work Regulations 1987* as amended

- Confined Spaces – *Confined Spaces Regulations 1997*

- Display Screens (VDUs) – *Health & Safety (Display Screen Equipment) Regulations 1992*

- Electricity – *Electricity at Work Regulations 1987*

- *Food Safety (General Food Hygiene) Regulations 1999*

- Hazardous Substances – *Control of Substances Hazardous to Health Regulations 1999 (COSHH)*

- Lead – *Control of Lead at Work Regulations 1998*

- Lifts and lifting – *Lifting Operations & Lifting Equipment Regulations 1998*

- Manual Handling – *Manual Handling Operations Regulations 1992*

- Noise – *Noise at Work Regulations 1989*

- Work Equipment – *Provision and Use of Work Equipment Regulations 1998*

- Workplace – *Workplace (Health, Safety & Welfare) Regulations 1992*

Notes:
(i) Some regulations, including some of those listed above, specifically call for an assessment to be carried out in respect to the risks associated with the subject of the regulation in question, for example the *Display Screen Equipment and Noise at Work Regulations*. Chapters 3 and 7 address regulations calling for special risk assessments.

(ii) All those involved with the risk assessment process cannot be expected to know of the existence of every regulation, although this knowledge should exist within the RAG in the person of the company competent health and safety adviser/s.

Codes of Practice and other guidance

4.18 Many regulations also have associated Approved Codes of Practice, and where they do these should be complied with. The HSC or HSE also publish a range of guidance notes on a wide variety of subjects. The requirements/standards of these codes and guidance should also be complied with unless the local arrangements provide a greater level of protection.

Although failure to comply with Approved Codes of Practice or guidance is not in itself an offence, failure to do so may be cited as proof of breach of relevant requirements in the event of prosecution. In such an event the onus would be upon a defendant company to demonstrate that what they did was as effective in affording protection as compliance with the code of practice or guidance.

The following is a non-exhaustive selection of such codes and guidance publications:

Free publications

—	INDG69	Violence to staff
—	INDG73	Working alone in safety
—	INDG84	Leptospirosis: are you at risk?
—	INDG175	Hand arm vibration: advice for employers
—	CAIS10	Ventilation of kitchens in catering establishments
—	FIS11	Priorities for health and safety in the poultry processing industry
—	DVIS 4	Compression chambers
—	CIS8	Safety in excavations
—	INDG169	Metalworking fluids and you
—	AS5	Farmers Lung
—	INDG226	Homeworking: guidance for employers and employees on health and safety
—	IACL27	Legionnaires Disease

Priced publications

—	HSG72	Control of respirable silica dust in heavy clay and refractory processes (1992)
—	HSG40	Chlorine from drums and cylinders (1987)
—	L27	The Control of Asbestos at Work: Control of Asbestos at Work Regulations 1987, Approved Code of Practice 3rd edition, (1999)
—	HSG118	Electrical safety in arc welding (1994)
—	HSG41	Petrol filling stations; construction and operation (1990)
—	HSG6	Safety in working with lift trucks (1997)
—	HSG154	Managing crowds safely

HSE Books publish catalogues of priced and free publications annually, and provide an advisory service on the latest position with regard to existing and proposed publications.

Catalogues, free and priced publications are available from HSE Books PO Box 1999 Sudbury Suffolk CO10 6FS Tel: 01787 881165, fax: 01787 313995.

Other standards

4.19 Other non-statutory standards include industry sector standards and standards established by individual firms or conglomerates for compliance by their subsidiaries.

Accident information

4.20   Any risk assessment developed without taking account of the accident statistics and records applicable to the process, area or subject of the risk assessment is, by definition, flawed.

Accident information is in most cases the most important aid to the risk assessment process, since it provides positive evidence of the existence of risks. The only exceptions to this rule will be smaller businesses where the number of reported accidents is small and therefore provides no indication of trends. This is one of the many reasons why every accident, however trivial, and irrespective of whether or not injuries resulted, should be reported, and why the company accident book or books should be reviewed by those responsible for risk assessments.

Important and useful information about workplace accidents is published annually in the Health and Safety Commissions 'Health and Safety Statistics'. Information in this document includes the total numbers of accidents by category, industry sector and major accident classifications. Copies of these statistics can also be obtained from HSE Books.

Employee input

4.21   *Regulation 12* of the *MHSWR* imposes a duty upon all employees to report serious or imminent danger, or other shortcomings in the company health and safety arrangements which they become aware of and which have the propensity to affect their health and safety at work. Such reports must be made to their employer or his nominated representative.

The implications of this duty insofar as risk assessment is concerned are clear, not only when risk assessments are being developed for the first time, but afterwards. Once a risk assessment has been developed and published, any employee report of serious or imminent danger or shortcoming in the health and safety arrangements implies a failure in the risk assessment process.

It might subsequently transpire that the perceived danger or shortcoming is unfounded or exaggerated, or that the risk could not reasonably have been detected or foreseen during the risk assessment process. Whatever the outcome, it is essential that any employee report in compliance with *regulation 12* is treated seriously, promptly investigated, and any implications for the risk assessment addressed.

Previous experience

4.22   Previous experience is not solely a matter of reviewing accident records. For many organisations there will be documented records of completed projects, from which lessons can be learned and improvements made.

This information will be important in the context of risk assessment. In many cases, for example in the construction industry and associated consultancies, project records and documentation are maintained, providing analysis of suitable construction materials and other important information. Such records became mandatory with the introduction of the *Construction (Design and Management) Regulations 1994.*

Competent Health and Safety Adviser

4.23   For many firms the statutory requirement in *regulation 6* of *MHSWR* to appoint one or more competent safety advisers to assist employers in discharging their health and safety responsibilities, was merely formalising what some employers had been doing for many years as a matter of good practice.

Nonetheless *regulation 6*, by requiring these appointments to be made in every business, recognises the fact that the volume and complexity of health and safety law is now such that employers need expertise at hand to advise them in complying with it.

As risk assessment is central to all health and safety activity, it follows that the health and safety adviser/s have a key role to play in this process. In this chapter it has been stated that these advisers should be included in the company Risk Assessment Group and that they should be able to highlight any regulation, code of practice or other guidance that exists pertaining to the work processes and operations of their employer.

In addition to these contributions to the process, health and safety advisers should also be available to give advice on every aspect of the risk assessment process, and should endorse every risk assessment before it is finally 'signed-off' for publication and implementation.

Checklist

4.24   Appendix A (at the end of this chapter) is a risk checklist which covers approximately 200 aspects of work activity classified by type of operation, activity or condition. Although no document of this nature can cover every risk in the workplace, this checklist covers specific work activities over a wide range of industry sectors as well as risks which could be present in all work situations.

Communications

4.25 Communications in the context of risk assessment are incredibly important. If all people at work have a part to play in the risk assessment process, they must all receive relevant and comprehensible information on the subject.

This means acquainting employees with details of the final risk assessment, and the measures taken to eliminate or reduce the risks identified, and much else.

Four key stages of the communication process

4.26 Although risk management related communications should be ongoing, there are four key stages of the risk assessment process at which communication is essential.

Stage 1: Before the initial risk assessment exercise commences

4.27 If the co-operation and input of employees is to be maximised, they need early warning that the process is about to begin. No point in their safety representative, manager or supervisor confronting them and asking for input without warning, and without time to give proper consideration to the matter.

Ideally the initial communication should explain the purpose and objective of risk assessment, the statutory requirement, how the process will operate, who is in the Risk Assessment Group, and most important, what the company programme/timetable is and the date when their input will be required.

If the initial communication is mishandled, there is likely to be a lukewarm or indifferent reaction.

Stage 2: Communication of details of the risk assessment and measures to eliminate or reduce the risks identified

4.28 This stage of the communication process is not an option, but a specific duty of employers within *regulation 3* of the *MHSWR*, which calls for communication of the significant findings of the risk assessment – as well as the measures taken to address the risks identified – to be communicated to every employee.

It might be convenient to publish a consolidated company risk assessment, providing a copy for each department and displaying the assessment on company notice boards.

This will be impractical for larger businesses because the document would be too large. In these cases each department, function or operation should hold an extract from the company risk assessment covering the part applicable to them, together with details of company-wide risks, ie those that apply to all employees irrespective of the work that they do. Where practicable a copy of this extract should be posted on department notice boards.

Stage 3: Reinforcement

4.29   The Company Safety Policy must include reference to risk assessment in Part III – arrangements to comply with the company policy on health and safety.

There are two key reasons for this:

(i)   The company Health and Safety Policy is the key reference point in respect to all health and safety matters. This means, *inter alia*, explaining what arrangements exist to create and maintain healthy and safe working practices and a healthy and safe working environment.

Clearly the policy will not meet this requirement if it does not include reference to the risk assessment.

(ii)   Inclusion of reference to risk assessment provides the opportunity to exhort employees to report any risks which they believe exist but which are not in the risk assessment.

The wording of the reference to risk assessment in their health and safety policy is a matter for each company to determine. The following example may be useful as a model:

'The company recognises the crucial role of risk assessment in creating and maintaining the highest standards of health and safety, and encourages the involvement of all employees in order to ensure that its risk assessments properly address all significant risks and identifies effective solutions to eliminate or mitigate these risks.

Our risk assessment was developed with the co-operation of employees, and every department has a copy of the latest version of the assessment applicable to them. A copy of the local assessment also appears on department notice boards together with the names and telephone numbers of the Company Risk Assessment group, who have responsibility for the management of our risk assessment programme.

However, a high level of risk management can only be sustained with the support of everyone in the company. If any member of staff believes that the current risk assessment does not cover every significant risk which they are aware of, or they subsequently become aware of new or emerging risks, they should report details at once to their health and safety representative, supervisor or manager.'

Stage 4: Special communication

4.30 In addition to the three key communication stages described, it is of course essential that all levels of management, and all health and safety representatives and members of the Risk Assessment Group receive suitable instruction and training covering all the matters in this chapter and in Chapter 5 – Risk Assessment Methodology.

Quick reference checklist for Chapter 4: Risk Assessment Preparation

Requirements	Relevant Paragraphs
If your company does not recognise Trade Unions, do the elected health and safety representatives have a role in the risk assessment process, including representation on the Risk Assessment Group or your equivalent of it?	4.6
Do line managers play a 'pro-active' role in the risk assessment process?	4.7
What precautions are taken to prevent 'Generic' risk assessments becoming the norm, in place of assessments generated locally and taking account of local conditions?	4.9
Is the organisation responsible for overseeing risk assessment activity in the company adequate, broadly representative and able to take a company-wide view?	4.10–4.13
Do you optimise the services of specialists when assessing risks?	4.13
Does your risk assessment steering group have available to it the various documentary aids which are important when considering risks?	4.16–4.20
Is there a procedure to facilitate the contribution/input of employees to the risk assessment process?	4.21
Does the company safety adviser 'sign-off' all risk assessments and is he/she co-opted onto the central risk assessment group or equivalent?	4.23
Are you satisfied that the quantity and quality of your in-house communications regarding risk assessment are adequate and calculated to maintain enthusiasm for risk assessment as a positive contributor to a safe and healthy working environment?	4.26–4.30

Appendix A — Non-exhaustive list of potential risks

This list is a combination of generic and specific aspects of work which could pose risks; it is not exhaustive. The purpose is to provide risk assessment groups with an *aide-mémoire* for use when preparing the list of risks applicable to the operations of their business or organisation.

For ease of reference the contents are arranged under the following headings, and within each group the risk areas are arranged alphabetically.

1. Electrical
2. Emergency response
3. Environment – general
4. Environment – working
5. Fire and explosion
6. Health
7. Mechanical
8. Permits to work
9. Personnel
10. Persons at particular risk
11. Place of work
12. Production
13. Security and violence
14. Substances materials

1. Electrical

Direct contact
Flash testing
Ignition source
Indirect contact
Overhead power lines
Portable tools
Short circuit/overload
Trailing leads
25 KV overhead

2. Emergency response

Emergency equipment missing/faulty
Emergency plan non-existent/outdated
Emergency vehicle access blocked
First-aid – none or insufficient

3. Environment – general

Discharge to drains

Disposal of waste
Drain overflow
Failure/inadequacy of bunds
Ground contamination
Noise nuisance
Solvent emissions
Spillages
Stack emissions

4. Environment – working

Ambient temperature
Cleanliness
Hot/cold surfaces
Humidity
Hygiene
Lighting (day & night)
Noise
Ventilation

5. Fire and explosion

Combustible waste
Electrical overload
Fire loading
Flammable atmospheres
Flammable dust
Flammable liquids
Gas cylinders
Ignition sources
Smoking/naked flame

6. Health

Dermatitis
Food poisoning
Hand/arm vibration syndrome
Hearing impairment
Ingestion of substances
Lasers
Legionella
Manual handling (back etc)
Microbiological
Radiation
Repetitive strain injury (RSI/WRULD)
Respiratory
Sensitisers

Sun rays
Vibration White Finger
Welding flash

7. Mechanical

Abrasion
Compressed air
Crushing
Cutting/shearing
Drawing-in/trapping
Entanglement
Flying particles
High pressure injection
High pressure systems
Impact
Lifting equipment
Lifting tackle failure
Machinery failures
Mobile equipment
Moving rail vehicles
Rotating shafts
Sharp surfaces
Stabbing
Vibrating

8. Permits to work

Effluent discharge consent
Environmental Protection Act 1990
Fire certificate
License to operate

9. Personnel (see also 10. Persons at particular risk)

Competent
Disabilities/restrictions
Fit
Hazardous behaviour (horseplay)
Informed

10. Persons at particular risk (see also 13. Security and violence)

Cleaners
Contractors
Disabled
Maintenance staff

Novices/new staff
Operatives
Postal staff
Pregnant staff
Receptionists
Security staff
Visitors
Young persons

Any employee working in isolation of other staff, or who works alone after normal working hours or during week-ends or public holidays.
When employees work at these times, their employer is under a greater duty of care than when they work normal hours alongside other employees.

11. Place of work

Access/egress
Confined spaces
Demolition
Fall of persons
Falling objects
High risk areas
Holes/pits
Housekeeping
Lack of oxygen
Movement – fork-lift trucks/vehicles
Obstructed gangways
Overhead cables
Overhead loads
Piped liquid and gas
Restricted height
Scaffolding/false work
Slips/trips
Stability of fixed equipment
Stability of workplace
Trench collapse
Underground cables
Working above liquids
Working at heights
Working near or above water

12. Production

Method of work (is system safe?)
Quality control

Software integrity
Storage of materials
Stored energy
Testing

13. Security and violence

Computer installation
Highly flammable vaults
High value items
Material stores
Money
Sensitive information
Substations (incoming services)

Violence – under this generic heading acts of violence may be generated/motivated for different reasons. It is therefore important for risk assessment groups to consider whether any of the causes/motivations could be present in their operations, for example:

- violence caused by frustration, e.g. passengers on transport systems;

- politically motivated violence (bombs, attacks on individuals);

- violence during robberies;

- violence as the by-product of acts of vandalism;

- violence induced by drugs/alcohol.

14. Substances/materials

Asbestos
Chemicals (*COSHH Regulations 1944*)
Dust/gases
Fumes/vapour/mist
Ionising radiations
Lead
Vehicle exhausts

5 Risk Assessment — Methodology

This chapter is in two parts as follows:
Part I – Methods of classifying risks
Part II – Managing risks following classification

Part I – Methods of classifying risks

Introduction

5.1 The statutory requirement for risk assessment does not call for risks to be evaluated and ranked in a particular way, although guidance to the regulations explains that the objective of 'ranking' is to ensure that focus is upon those risks which have the greatest potential for harm. Without some form of 'ranking' or classification, time and resource might be spent concentrating on risks which do not pose a significant threat.

Neither the regulations or their associated guidance specify how risk ranking is to be carried out, and this has resulted in the development of a variety of methods of doing so, ranging from the basic/intuitive to calculated/high tech. This chapter examines methods evolved for assessing/ranking risks.

Definition of risk – what is risk?

5.2 Risk in the context in which it is used in *regulation 3* of *MHSWR* is the sum of two essential considerations, those of probability (or likelihood or frequency) and consequences (or severity of outcome) of an unplanned and unwelcome event.

There is a significant difference between a risk where the probability of occurrence is high but the consequences of the event would be low, compared to a risk where the likelihood of occurrence is high and the consequences also high. Such differences give rise to the need to assess or rank risks.

The definition of risk can therefore be expressed as follows:

$$\text{RISK} = \frac{\text{Hazard severity/seriousness}}{\text{(potential for harm/loss)}} \times \frac{\text{Likelihood/probability}}{\text{(of occurrence)}}$$

The purpose of statutory risk assessment is to determine the likelihood of events and their consequences in relation to the operations of the enterprise in question, insofar as they could affect employees and others not employed by those carrying out the risk assessment.

The objective of this handbook is to assist employers and those concerned with the development and maintenance of risk assessments to comply with *regulation 3* of *MHSWR*.

Although *regulation 3* is concerned only with risks to people, the risk spectrum in the business environment includes all risks which could affect the commercial viability of an enterprise, although commercial risks are not within the remit of this handbook.

Risk assessment methods

5.3 Three quite different generic methods of carrying out risk assessment are described. There are a number of permutations of these methods, especially so in respect to the '5×5' method.

(a) Basic/intuitive

This simple method of assessment is suited to small businesses whose operations are uncomplicated and which present few risks, for example commercial offices employing less than ten people.

In such businesses the use of display screen equipment will present some risks and there could be some potentially hazardous manual handling. However, both these risks categories and the measure to mitigate tem are addressed by eponymous regulations relating to these operations, and in each case they have to be considered as a separate exercise as described in Chapter 3.

For the small firm a simple risk assessment method can be justified by the relatively risk-free nature of the operations, the small number of employees and the fact that usually no clear patterns or causative trends can be discerned from the few accidents recorded in the statutory accident record book.

The method followed is one where those responsible for the risk assessment, having brainstormed or used other methods of listing all the potential risks, including taking account of input from workers or their representatives, then work through the list assigning a classification of 'Low', 'Medium' or 'High' to each risk, according to the majority view of those involved in the assessment.

5.4   Risk Assessment — Methodology

Clearly this system relies heavily upon the knowledge and/or experience of the assessment group or team, and of all the methods used for assessing risks, this is the most subjective. Nonetheless, if the size and nature of a companies operations are as described, it must be a 'suitable and sufficient' method of assessing risks.

(b) The '5×5' method of assessment

This method, even in its most basic form, applies a more structured and quantified approach to risk assessment than the basic/intuitive method described above.

The 5×5 method or principle and derivatives of it are by far the most common method of risk assessment used, no doubt because it requires a degree of careful consideration without getting into high technology.

This method has as its basis the allocation of a numeric value to the two elements of the equation (likelihood and severity), so that the risk equation becomes a simple mathematical one.

Both elements (likelihood and severity) are assigned a value on a scale from one to five, and the two resultant numbers are then multiplied, thereby producing a unique total value or score between 1 and 25 for each risk considered. (See Figure 1.)

The unique numerical score of each risk enables it to be categorised as 'High', 'Medium' or 'Low' – see Table 1. In some cases, in order to indicate that no action of any kind will be taken in respect to a particular risk, a fourth classification 'no further action' might be used.

Although the actions to be taken to remove or ameliorate the risks identified, irrespective of their unique number and subsequent categorisation, are likely to be different in each case, it follows that there must be some basic parameters of action for each category. Table 2 describes these parameters.

Improvements to the basic '5×5' assessment method

5.4   Figure 1 shows a basic '5×5' model designed to provide a more structured risk assessment than that described in paragraph 5.3(a), which is intuitive and highly subjective.

The purpose of this paragraph is to consider improvements to the basic '5×5' approach shown in Figure 1, by specifying criteria for assigning numerical values for likelihood and severity.

Table 1 – Recommended numerical parameters of the three categories of risk

Score	Category
Below 8	Low risk
9–15	Medium risk
16–25	High risk

Notes:

(i) If considered necessary, a further grouping 'no further action' could be used for risks whose score is up to and including 4.

(ii) The numerical parameters for each group are not defined in regulations, and are a matter for risk assessors to determine. Provided that the numerical criteria decided upon is applied consistently by those involved in the assessment process, this should satisfy the 'Suitable and sufficient' qualification in *regulation 3* of *MHSWR*.

Table 2 – Requirements for action – High, Medium and Low categories of risk

Category	Action required
High risk	Immediate action necessary to reduce to 'Medium' or below. Serious consideration to be given to stopping the operation, or applying temporary restriction of full operation pending outcome of evaluation of options for reducing the risk level. Urgency is emphasised; action on risk in this category cannot be deferred/put on hold, etc.
Medium risks	Situation is not acceptable and should be improved; objective should be to re-categorise as 'Low' as soon as possible. Unlikely to require the operations in question to be stopped.
Low risks	Objective should be to eliminate the risk if possible, or to make further reductions in the risk value where reasonably practicable.

Likelihood

The following applies where consideration is of the probability/ likelihood of injuries resulting from the risk being evaluated.

Injury likely to occur daily = 5
              weekly = 4
              monthly = 3
              four times a year = 2
              once a year = 1

A number of permutations of these frequencies are possible. An important aid when applying this method of quantification is previous experience; this can be obtained from company accident report books or figures derived from them.

5.4 Risk Assessment — Methodology

Figure 1 Basic 5×5 method of risk assessment/evaluation

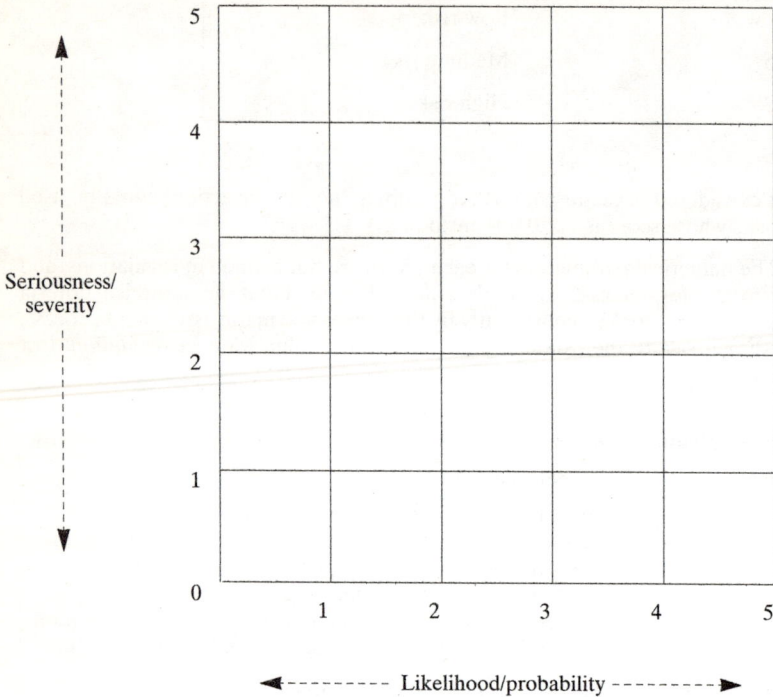

The above frequencies can also be used by firms whose risk assessment has to take account of the possibility of reportable diseases arising from the nature of their operations. A schedule of these diseases, which are taken from *RIDDOR 1995*, is in Table 3. However, employers cannot predict the seriousness of a reportable disease, therefore the severity/seriousness table in the following paragraph cannot be used for calculating the unique risk values of risks connected with diseases which might have to be included in a risk assessment.

In most cases, however, workplace diseases which are reportable arise from work tasks which are already the subject of legislation, for example the *Control of Substances Hazardous to Health Regulations 1999 (COSHH)*, and will therefore be addressed in the measures necessary to comply with such regulations.

Given the relatively small number of disease conditions which are not addressed by their own unique regulations, it is recommended that other 'disease' risks are assigned the maximum score (5) for seriousness.

Table 3 – Schedule 3 Reportable diseases

Regulation 5
Part I Occupational diseases (Guidance is given at Paragraph 159 on those items marked with an asterisk)

Diseases	Activities
Conditions due to physical agents and the physical demands of work	
1* Inflammation, ulceration or malignant disease of the skin due to ionising radiation.	Work with ionising radiation.
2* Malignant disease of the bones due to ionising radiation.	
3* Blood dyscrasia due to ionising radiation.	
4* Cataract due to electromagnetic radiation.	Work involving exposure to electromagnetic radiation (including radiant heat).
5* Decompression illness.	Work involving breathing gases at increased pressure (including diving).
6 Barotrauma resulting in lung or other organ damage.	
7 Dysbaric osteonecrosis.	
8* Cramp of the hand or forearm due to repetitive movements.	Work involving prolonged periods of handwriting, typing or other repetitive movements of the fingers, hand or arm.
9 Subcutaneous cellulitis of the hand (beat hand).	Physically demanding work causing severe or prolonged friction or pressure on the hand.
10 Bursitis or subcutaneous cellulitis arising at or about the knee due to severe or prolonged external friction or pressure at or about the knee (beat knee).	Physically demanding work causing severe or prolonged friction or pressure at or about the knee.
11 Bursitis or subcutaneous cellulitis arising at or about the elbow due to severe or prolonged external friction or pressure at or about the elbow (beat elbow).	Physically demanding work causing severe or prolonged friction or pressure at or about the elbow.
12 Traumatic inflammation of the tendons of the hand or forearm or of the associated tendon sheaths.	Physically demanding work, frequent or repeated movements, constrained postures or extremes of extension or flexion of the hand or wrist.
13 Carpal tunnel syndrome.	Work involving the use of hand-held vibrating tools.
14* Hand-arm vibration syndrome.	Work involving: (a) the use of chain saws, brush cutters or hand-held or hand-fed circular saws in forestry or woodworking;

Diseases	Activities
	(b) the use of hand-held rotary tools in grinding material or in sanding or polishing metal;
	(c) the holding of material being ground or metal being sanded or polished by rotary tools;
	(d) the use of hand-held percussive metal-working tools or the holding of metal being worked upon by percussive tools in connection with riveting, caulking, chipping, hammering, fettling or swaging;
	(e) the use of hand-held powered percussive drills or hand-held powered percussive hammers in mining, quarrying or demolition, or on roads or footpaths (including road construction); or
	(f) the holding of material being worked upon by pounding machines in shoe manufacture.
Infections due to biological agents	
15 Anthrax.	(a) Work involving handling infected animals, their products or packaging containing infected material; or
	(b) work on infected sites.
16 Brucellosis.	Work involving contact with:
	(a) animals or their carcasses (including any parts thereof) infected by brucella or the untreated products of same; or
	(b) laboratory specimens or vaccines of or containing brucella.
17 (a) Avian chlamydiosis.	Work involving contact with birds infected with chlamydia psittaci, or the remains or untreated products of such birds.
(b) Ovine chlamydiosis.	Work involving contact with sheep infected with chlamydia psittaci, or the remains or untreated products of such sheep.

Diseases	Activities
18* Hepatitis.	Work involving contact with: (a) human blood or human blood products; or (b) any source of viral hepatitis.
19 Legionellosis.	Work on or near cooling systems which are located in the workplace and use water; or work on hot water service systems located in the workplace which are likely to be a source of contamination.
20 Leptospirosis.	(a) Work in places which are or are liable to be infested by rats, fieldmice, voles or other small mammals; (b) work at dog kennels or involving the care or handling of dogs; or (c) work involving contact with bovine animals or their meat products or pigs or their meat products.
21 Lyme disease.	Work involving exposure to ticks (including in particular work by forestry workers, rangers, dairy farmers, game keepers and other persons engaged in countryside management).
22 Q fever.	Work involving contact with animals, their remains or their untreated products.
23 Rabies.	Work involving handling or contact with infected animals.
24 Streptococcus suis.	Work involving contact with pigs infected with streptococcus suis, or with the carcasses, products or residues of pigs so affected.
25 Tetanus.	Work involving contact with soil likely to be contaminated by animals.
26 Tuberculosis.	Work with persons, animals, human or animal remains or any other material which might be a source of infection.
27 Any infection reliably attributable to the performance of the work specified in the entry opposite hereto.	Work with micro-organisms; work with live or dead human beings in the course of providing any treatment or service or in conducting any investigation involving exposure to blood or body fluids; work with animals or any potentially infected material derived from any of the above.

5.4   Risk Assessment — Methodology

Diseases	Activities
Conditions due to substances	
28 Poisonings by any of the following: (a) acrylamide monomer; (b) arsenic or one of its compounds; (c) benzene or a homologue of benzene; (d) beryllium or one of its compounds; (e) cadmium or one of its compounds; (f) carbon disulphide; (g) diethylene dioxide (dioxan); (h) ethylene oxide; (i) lead or one of its compounds; (j) manganese or one of its compounds; (k) mercury or one of its compounds; (l) methyl bromide; (m) nitrochlorobenzene, or a nitro- or amino- or chloro-derivative of benzene or of a homologue of benzene; (n) oxides of nitrogen; (o) phosphorus or one of its compounds.	Any activity.
29 Cancer of a bronchus or lung.	(a) Work in or about a building where nickel is produced by decomposition of a gaseous nickel compound or where any industrial process which is ancillary or incidental to that process is carried on; or (b) work involving exposure to bis (chloromethyl) ether or any electrolytic chromium processes (excluding passivation) which involve hexavalent chromium compounds, chromate production or zinc chromate pigment manufacture.
30 Primary carcinoma of the lung where there is accompanying evidence of silicosis.	Any occupation in: (a) glass manufacture; (b) sandstone tunnelling or quarrying; (c) the pottery industry;

Diseases	Activities
	(d) metal ore mining;
	(e) slate quarrying or slate production;
	(f) clay mining;
	(g) the use of siliceous materials as abrasives;
	(h) foundry work;
	(i) granite tunnelling or quarrying; or
	(j) stone cutting or masonry.
31 Cancer of the urinary tract.	1 Work involving exposure to any of the following substances:
	(a) beta-naphthylamine or methylene-bis-orthochloroaniline;
	(b) diphenyl substituted by at least one nitro or primary amino group or by at least one nitro and primary amino group (including benzidine);
	(c) any of the substances mentioned in sub-paragraph (b) above if further ring substituted by halogeno, methyl or methoxy groups, but not by other groups; or
	(d) the salts of any of the substances mentioned in sub-paragraphs (a) to (c) above.
	2 The manufacture of auramine or magenta.
32 Bladder cancer.	Work involving exposure to aluminium smelting using the Soderberg process.
33 Angiosarcoma of the liver.	(a) Work in or about machinery or apparatus used for the polymerisation of vinyl chloride monomer, a process which, for the purposes of this sub-paragraph, comprises all operations up to and including the drying of the slurry produced by the polymerisation and the packaging of the dried product; or

107

5.4   Risk Assessment — Methodology

Diseases	Activities
	(b) work in a building or structure in which any part of the process referred to in the foregoing sub-paragraph takes place.
34 Peripheral neuropathy.	Work involving the use or handling of or exposure to the fumes of or vapour containing n-hexane or methyl n-butyl ketone.
35 Chrome ulceration of: (a) the nose or throat; or (b) the skin of the hands or forearm.	Work involving exposure to chromic acid or to any other chromium compound.
36 Folliculitis. 37 Acne. 38 Skin cancer. 39 Pneumoconiosis (excluding asbestosis).	Work involving exposure to mineral oil, tar, pitch or arsenic. 1 (a) The mining, quarrying or working of silica rock or the working of dried quartzose sand, any dry deposit or residue of silica or any dry admixture containing such materials (including any activity in which any of the aforesaid operations are carried out incidentally to the mining or quarrying of other minerals or to the manufacture of articles containing crushed or ground silica rock); or (b) the handling of any of the materials specified in the foregoing sub-paragraph in or incidentally to any of the operations mentioned therein or substantial exposure to the dust arising from such operations. 2 The breaking, crushing or grinding of flint, the working or handling of broken, crushed or ground flint or materials containing such flint or substantial exposure

Diseases		*Activities*
		to the dust arising from any of such operations.
	3	Sand blasting by means of compressed air with the use of quartzose sand or crushed silica rock or flint or substantial exposure to the dust arising from such sand blasting.
	4	Work in a foundry or the performance of, or substantial exposure to the dust arising from, any of the following operations:
		(a) the freeing of steel castings from adherent siliceous substance; or
		(b) the freeing of metal castings from adherent siliceous substance:
		(i) by blasting with an abrasive propelled by compressed air, steam or a wheel, or
		(ii) by the use of power-driven tools.
	5	The manufacture of china or earthenware (including sanitary earthenware, electrical earthenware and earthenware tiles) and any activity involving substantial exposure to the dust arising therefrom.
	6	The grinding of mineral graphite or substantial exposure to the dust arising from such grinding.
	7	The dressing of granite or any igneous rock by masons, the crushing of such materials or substantial exposure to the dust arising from such operations.
	8	The use or preparation for use of an abrasive wheel or substantial exposure to the dust arising therefrom.

Diseases	Activities
	9 (a) Work underground in any mine in which one of the objects of the mining operations is the getting of any material;
	(b) the working or handling above ground at any coal or tin mine of any materials extracted therefrom or any operation incidental thereto;
	(c) the trimming of coal in any ship, barge, lighter, dock or harbour or at any wharf or quay; or
	(d) the sawing, splitting or dressing of slate or any operation incidental thereto.
	10 The manufacture or work incidental to the manufacture of carbon electrodes by an industrial undertaking for use in the electrolytic extraction of aluminium from aluminium oxide and any activity involving substantial exposure to the dust therefrom.
	11 Boiler scaling or substantial exposure to the dust arising therefrom.
40 Byssinosis.	The spinning or manipulation of raw or waste cotton or flax or the weaving of cotton or flax, carried out in each case in a room in a factory, together with any other work carried out in such a room.
41 Mesothelioma 42 Lung cancer 43 Asbestosis	(a) The working or handling of asbestos or any admixture of asbestos;
	(b) the manufacture or repair of asbestos textiles or other articles containing or composed of asbestos;

Diseases	Activities
	(c) the cleaning of any machinery or plant used in any of the foregoing operations and of any chambers, fixtures and appliances for the collection of asbestos dust; or
	(d) substantial exposure to the dust arising from any of the foregoing operations.
44 Cancer of the nasal cavity or associated air sinuses.	1 (a) Work in or about a building where wooden furniture is manufactured;
	(b) work in a building used for the manufacture of footwear or components of footwear made wholly or partly of leather or fibre board; or
	(c) work at a place used wholly or mainly for the repair of footwear made wholly or partly of leather or fibre board.
	2 Work in or about a factory building where nickel is produced by decomposition of a gaseous nickel compound or in any process which is ancillary or incidental thereto.
45* Occupational dermatitis.	Work involving exposure to any of the following agents:
	(a) epoxy resin systems;
	(b) formaldehyde and its resins;
	(c) metalworking fluids;
	(d) chromate (hexavalent and derived from trivalent chromium);
	(e) cement, plaster or concrete;
	(f) acrylates and methacrylates;
	(g) colophony (rosin) and its modified products;
	(h) glutaraldehyde;

5.4   Risk Assessment — Methodology

Diseases	Activities
	(i) mercaptobenzothiazole, thiurams, substituted paraphenylene-diamines and related rubber processing chemicals;
	(j) biocides, anti-bacterials, preservatives or disinfectants;
	(k) organic solvents;
	(l) antibiotics and other pharmaceuticals and therapeutic agents;
	(m) strong acids, strong alkalis, strong solutions (eg brine) and oxidising agents including domestic bleach or reducing agents;
	(n) hairdressing products including in particular dyes, shampoos, bleaches and permanent waving solutions;
	(o) soaps and detergents;
	(p) plants and plant-derived material including in particular especially the daffodil, tulip and chrysanthemum families, the parsley family (carrots, parsnips, parsley and celery), garlic and onion, hardwoods and the pine family;
	(q) fish, shell-fish or meat;
	(r) sugar or flour; or
	(s) any other known irritant or sensitising agent including in particular any chemical bearing the warning 'may cause sensitisation by skin contact' or 'irritating to the skin'.
46 Extrinsic alveolitis (including farmer's lung).	Exposure to moulds, fungal spores or heterologous proteins during work in:
	(a) agriculture, horticulture, forestry, cultivation of edible fungi or malt-working;
	(b) loading, unloading or handling mouldy vegetable matter or edible fungi whilst same is being stored;

Diseases	Activities
	(c) caring for or handling birds; or
	(d) handling bagasse.
47* Occupational asthma.	Work involving exposure to any of the following agents:
	(a) isocyanates;
	(b) platinum salts;
	(c) fumes or dust arising from the manufacture, transport or use of hardening agents (including epoxy resin curing agents) based on phthalic anhydride, tetrachlorophthalic anhydride, trimellitic anhydride or triethylene-tetramine;
	(d) fumes arising from the use of rosin as a soldering flux;
	(e) proteolytic enzymes;
	(f) animals including insects and other arthropods used for the purposes of research or education or in laboratories;
	(g) dusts arising from the sowing, cultivation, harvesting, drying, handling, milling, transport or storage of barley, oats, rye, wheat or maize or the handling, milling, transport or storage of meal or flour made therefrom;
	(h) antibiotics;
	(i) cimetidine;
	(j) wood dust;
	(k) ispaghula;
	(l) castor bean dust;
	(m) ipecacuanha;
	(n) azodicarbonamide;
	(o) animals including insects and other arthropods (whether in their larval forms or not) used for the purposes of pest control or fruit cultivation or the larval forms of animals used for the purposes of research or education or in laboratories;
	(p) glutaraldehyde;

Diseases	Activities	
	(q)	persulphate salts or henna;
	(r)	crustaceans or fish or products arising from these in the food processing industry;
	(s)	reactive dyes;
	(t)	soya bean;
	(u)	tea dust;
	(v)	green coffee bean dust;
	(w)	fumes from stainless steel welding;
	(x)	any other sensitising agent, including in particular any chemical bearing the warning 'may cause sensitisation by inhalation'.

Guidance on diseases/conditions in Schedule 3, Part I

The following table gives notes on those diseases in Schedule 3, Part I which have been highlighted with an asterisk.

Disease/condition	Schedule 3, Part I, Item No	Guidance
Inflammation, ulceration or malignant disease of the skin due to ionising radiation	1	The following conditions should always be reported under this heading: • erythema, primary or secondary radiation burns; • subsequent acute or chronic ulcers. Non melanoma skin cancer is common in the general population. It need only be reported if the history of exposure or the features of the condition suggest an association with ionising radiation. This would be the case in respect of: • squamous cell carcinoma occurring after high-dose exposure or at the site of past ulceration; • basal cell carcinoma where features such as multiple lesions suggest a possible relationship with ionising radiation.

Disease/condition	Schedule 3, Part I, Item No	Guidance
Malignant disease of the bones due to ionising radiation	2	Sarcoma of the bone is reportable. Secondary malignant disease of the bone is not reportable.
Blood dyscrasia due to ionising radiation	3	The following conditions are reportable: • acute changes in the blood picture, eg reduction in the number of small lymphocytes where no other clinical causes are established and there is reason to believe that this is the result of acute exposure to ionising radiation; • acute leukemia's; • chronic myeloid leukemia; • Non-Hodgkins lymphoma; • aplastic anaemia. Polycythaemia rubra vera is not reportable.
Cataract due to electromagnetic radiation	4	Cataracts are common in the general population. They need not be reported where there is good reason to believe that they were not caused at work by exposure to electromagnetic radiation (eg ionising radiation, microwaves). Cataracts resulting from exposure to ionising radiations or to radiant heat typically occur at the posterior pole of the lens. Intense exposure to microwave radiation may result in anterior or posterior subcapsular opacities.
Decompression illness	5	Decompression illness is defined as any signs or symptoms arising from the presence of gas within tissues or vessels of the body following a reduction in ambient pressure.

Disease/condition	Schedule 3, Part I, Item No	Guidance
Cramp of the hand or forearm due to repetitive movements	8	Cramp is reportable where it is a chronic condition linked to repetitive work movements. The condition is usually characterised by the inability to carry out a sequence of what were previously well co-ordinated movements. An acute incident of cramp which may occur in the course of work is not reportable.
Hand-arm vibration syndrome (HAVS)	14	Workers whose hands are regularly exposed to high vibration, for example in industries where vibratory tools and machines are used, may suffer from several kinds of injury to the hands and arm including impaired blood circulation and damage to the nerves and muscles. The injuries collectively are known as 'hand-arm vibration syndrome'. Other names used in industry include – vibration white finger, dead finger, dead hand and white finger. The severity of the vascular and neurological effects is indicated using an agreed classification system, the Stockholm Workshop Scales. More information on this and HAVS is contained in HSE guidance *Hand-arm vibration*[8].
Hepatitis	18	The likely sources of hepatitis are: Hepatitis A and E – human excreta and objects and consumables contaminated principally by excreta from people infected with hepatitis A or E virus. Hepatitis B, C and D – human blood and body fluids from people infected with hepatitis viruses B, C and D*,

Disease/condition	Schedule 3, Part I, Item No	Guidance
		objects contaminated by blood and body fluids, particularly sharp objects such as used hypodermic needles, contaminated broken glassware and other items where these penetrate the skin or otherwise may act as a vehicle for transmission of infection. Other, as yet uncharacterised, forms of viral hepatitis are known to exist. * hepatitis D virus is only infectious in the presence of concomitant or pre-existing infection with hepatitis B.
Any infection reliably attributable to the performance of the work specified opposite hereto	27	Many minor infections such as those causing bouts of diarrhoea and respiratory complaints such as colds and bronchitis are common in the community and everyone is exposed to them. These minor illnesses cannot generally be attributed to infection contracted at work and they are generally not reportable. However, where there is reasonable circumstantial evidence, for example, known contact with the infectious agent in laboratory work, a report should be made.
Occupational dermatitis	45	Item 45 (s) – any other known irritant or sensitising agent. A list of examples of 'other known irritants or sensitising agents' is given in Appendix 1 of HSE Guidance Note MS 24, Health Surveillance of Occupational Skin Disease[9], and further guidance is available in the references provided in Appendix 3 of the document.

Disease/condition	Schedule 3, Part I, Item No	Guidance
Occupational asthma	47	Dermatitis can be caused by exposure to a range of common agents found outside the workplace. If there is good evidence that the condition has been caused solely by such exposure rather than by exposure to an agent at work it need not be reported. Item 47(x) – any other sensitising agent. For examples of agents reported to have caused occupational asthma see Preventing Asthma at Work – How to Control Respiratory Sensitisers[10]. Asthma is a common condition in the general population. If there is good evidence that the condition: • was pre-existing and/or; • has been caused solely by exposure to agents outside work; and • was neither exacerbated nor triggered by exposure at work, the condition need not be reported.

Regulation 5

Part II Diseases additionally reportable in respect of offshore workplaces

48   Chickenpox.
49   Cholera.
50   Diptheria.
51   Dysentery (amoebic or bacillary).
52   Acute encephalitis.
53   Erysipelas.
54   Food Poisoning.
55   Legionellosis.
56   Malaria.
57   Measles.
58   Meningitis.
59   Meningococcal septicaemia (without meningitis).
60   Mumps.
61   Paratyphoid fever.
62   Plague.

63   Acute poliomyelitis.
64   Rabies.
65   Rubella.
66   Scarlet fever.
67   Tetanus.
68   Tuberculosis.
69   Typhoid fever.
70   Typhus.
71   Viral haemorrhagic fevers.
72   Viral hepatitis.

Severity/seriousness

The statutory accident etc reporting regulations are the *Reporting of Injuries, Diseases and Dangerous Occurrences Regulations 1995 (RIDDOR)*, which call for the reporting of fatal injuries and a number of other injuries (see Table 4) and these regulations provide standards for 2 of the 5 categories of severity shown below insofar as workplace injuries are concerned.

Fatal and multi-fatal = 5
Serious injury as defined in *RIDDOR* = 4
3-day injury as defined in *RIDDOR* = 3
Injury treated as 'first-aid' only injury = 2
Injury not requiring first-aid = 1

Unlike the frequency definitions, and given that the 'seriousness' categories are derived from the *RIDDOR* regulations, permuta-

Table 4 – Schedule 1 Major Injuries

1   Any fracture, other than to the fingers, thumbs or toes.
2   Any amputation.
3   Dislocation of the shoulder, hip, knee or spine.
4   Loss of sight (whether temporary or permanent).
5   A chemical or hot metal burn to the eye or any penetrating injury to the eye.
6   Any injury resulting from an electric shock or electrical burn (including any electrical burn caused by arcing or arcing products) leading to unconsciousness or requiring resuscitation or admittance to hospital for more than 24 hours.
7   Any other injury – (a)   leading to hypothermia, heat-induced illness or to unconsciousness, (b)   requiring resuscitation, or (c)   requiring admittance to hospital for more than 24 hours.
8   Loss of consciousness caused by asphyxia or by exposure to a harmful substance or biological agent.
9   Either of the following conditions which result from the absorption of any substance by inhalation, ingestion or through the skin –

(a)   acute illness requiring medical treatment; or

(b)   loss of consciousness.

10   Acute illness which requires medical treatment where there is reason to believe that this resulted from exposure to a biological agent or its toxins or infected material.

- The following notes explain some of the main terms used:

(a)   fracture includes a break, crack or chip;

(b)   amputation means either traumatic amputation at the time of the accident or surgical amputation following the accident (but the latter is more likely to be covered by 7(c));

(c)   requiring admittance to hospital for more than 24 hours includes situations where, had the injured person not already been in hospital, the injury would have resulted in admission for more than 24 hours;

(d)   acute illness means illness which:

　　(i)   progresses rapidly to a crisis after the onset of symptoms: and

　　(ii)   has severe symptoms;

(e)   medical treatment covers hospital treatment, treatment by a general medical practitioner, or treatment by a firm's medical and nursing staff;

(f)   loss of consciousness means the injured person enters into a state, for however short a period, where there is a lack of response, either vocal or physical, to people trying to communicate with them;

(g)   biological agent is defined in the Control of Substances Hazardous to Health Regulations 1999 as meaning 'any micro-organism, cell culture, or human endoparasite including any which have been genetically modified, which may cause any infection, allergy, toxicity or otherwise create a risk to human health'. In the context of the infection hazards relevant to RIDDOR 1995 this will in practice cover bacteria, viruses, fungi and parasites.

- The following notes indicate the kinds of accidents which can lead to the reportable health conditions included in the list of major injuries:

(a)   loss of consciousness resulting from asphyxia (lack of oxygen):

　　(i)   entry of a person into a confined space containing an oxygen deficient atmosphere;

　　(ii)   failure of air or oxygen supply in breathing apparatus

(b)   acute illness (absorption of any substance):

　　(i)   overturning, collapse or bursting of something containing a toxic substance, causing a spillage which contaminates the working environment;

　　(ii)   handling of surfaces of plant, containers etc, onto which a skin absorbable toxic substance had leaked without the knowledge of the person affected;

　　(iii) use or handling of material containing a toxic substance, the presence of which was not known, in a way which led to an episode of high exposure to that substance;

　　(iv)   an unexpected reaction between chemical compounds giving off a toxic gas or vapour which contaminates the working environment;

　　(v)   inadvertent or unknowing entry of a person into a confined space containing a toxic gas or vapour;

(c)   acute illness (exposure to a biological agent or its toxins or infected material):

(i) escape or release of a biological agent or its toxins or infected material into a working environment by, for example, the failure of a fermenter or a centrifuge, breakage of a flask, a spillage, filter failure;

(ii) exposure to a biological agent or its toxins or infected material through, for example, accidental self-inoculation (eg by the needle of a syringe or other contaminated sharp item), animal bite or laceration.

tions of the above are unlikely to provide a more accurate basis for assessment.

Technical methods of assessment

5.5 Intuitive and '5×5' methods of assessment have been discussed. The third and final group of assessment methods are intended to produce assessments which are developed by following a more disciplined and structured appraisal of risks. These methods are not appropriate or necessary for the majority of businesses.

For high risk industries such as the petro-chemical sector, use of one or more of the techniques briefly described might be necessary to demonstrate that the risk assessment process has been 'suitable and sufficient'.

(i) Failure Modes and Effects Analysis (FMEA)

The approach of FMEA is that of a systematic evaluation to examine the safety of a system by considering all the possible failure modes of every component. This approach is often referred to as a 'Bottom-up' technique, the opposite being the 'top down' method known as Fault Tree Analysis (see below).

FMEA has the advantage that it is thorough, although extremely time consuming and requiring the production of huge quantities of documents and technical information, and is hardware orientated.

(ii) Fault Tree Analysis (FTA)

FTA is based on a logical diagrammatic presentation of failures required to produce a particular hazard. Results in the display of combination failures. Works on the principle that major failure modes in the system under consideration ('Top Events') are shown, then all the possible causes of such events are considered.

The completed 'tree' is a pictorial aid to recognising and understanding the interdependencies of failure modes of the system. FTA is also time consuming and requires a highly skilled team leader to co-ordinate.

(iii) Hazard and Operability Study (HAZOP)

This method is colloquially referred to as the 'what if?' approach.

It involves the systematic analysis of each component to assess the failure potential and determine what adverse effects could arise from every deviation from the normal.

Those involved must be knowledgeable with regard to the system and the team leader should understand the principles of HAZOP.

The effectiveness of HAZOP is dependant on the level of knowledge and experience of the team members; it is not a technique which benefits from the incorporation into the team of 'fresh minds' since real-time experience of the system is an essential pre-requisite of those involved.

Training

5.6   Training in each of the techniques discussed in paragraph 5.5, while not essential, will improve the contribution of all of those involved. The following offer training courses:

Institution of Chemical Engineers (IChemE)
165–189 Railway Terrace
Rugby CV21 3HQ

Tel: 01788 578214
Fax: 01788 560833

COSH Services
Beckermet
Cumbria CA21 21F

Tel: 01946 841660

Summary

5.7   Those responsible for developing risk assessments, whether at local or company/organisation level, must be clear about the method of assessment which is to be used. In many firms, the '5×5' method has been taken as a basis and then modified to make it more appropriate to the firms operations. Examples of such modifications appear in Appendix A at the end of this chapter.

Care must be taken to ensure that every aspect of a task or series of tasks are taken into account. It is recommended that those responsible for developing risk assessments actually visit the site of each risk being considered, to be shown at 'first-hand' precisely what takes place. This approach frequently reveals minor aspects of a task or process which pose risks, even though the generally held view may be that the entire task/operation is without risk.

While there are possible risks associated with a wide variety of work processes, there are two categories in the schedule – 'Personnel' and 'Persons particularly at risk' – which apply across the entire spectrum of work, and these must always be kept in mind during the assessment process. Among those listed in the latter category are pregnant women and young people; special care should therefore be taken to ensure that potential risks to these two groups are carefully analysed – see Chapter 7.

The *Management of Health and Safety at Work Regulations 1992* (*MHSWR*) have been amended since 1992 to specifically demand that a risk assessment be conducted, or an existing assessment reviewed, in the event the work under consideration is to be done by a pregnant employee or a young person.

A recent judgement has established that it is necessary for those carrying out risk assessments to take account of the 'possibility' of pregnant women carrying out the tasks, in advance of it happening – see Chapter 9, paragraph 9.5–1.

It is also important to emphasise that the statutory requirement in relation to risk assessment embraces mental as well as physical considerations; this is acknowledged to be a difficult area, and one requiring considerably more research and wider understanding.

There are currently no laws dealing specifically with this subject, although the requirement to undertake risk assessments when work is to be done by young people emphasises the need to consider the psychological capacity of young persons (see Chapter 7, paragraph 7.7).

There is currently a consultation exercise in process which could lead to better guidance, publication of an Approved Code of Practice or even regulations specific to this subject. Meantime those involved in risk assessments should be aware of the potential for some work tasks to create stress, and to identify and consider this as part of the overall assessment process.

Part II – Managing risks following classification

Introduction

5.8   When the risk evaluation process has been completed, the task of managing or controlling the evaluated risks must begin. Since 1993 a considerable amount of guidance has appeared dealing with risk control, much of it derived from basic principles which are generally referred to as 'the hierarchy of measures'.

The hierarchy of measures are a set of logical actions and considerations, the first two of which (avoidance or elimination and combating risks at source) are sequential. These measures follow.

Avoidance/elimination of risk

Examples

5.9   (i)   If a substance currently in use poses health risks, is there a viable alternative which is less harmful? In recent years there has been significant progress in the introduction of harmless or less harmful substitutes for those substances with hazardous characteristics.

   (ii)   Individuals working alone after normal hours or at weekends, must, by definition, be at greater risk than when working alongside colleagues during normal business hours. If this practice is stopped, the risk is removed at once, and without the need for elaborate and expensive arrangements to check on the well-being of staff who work at unusual times.

   Clearly the option to prohibit working by lone individuals outside normal hours cannot be applied universally.

Combating risks at source

Examples

5.10   (i)   Better to ensure effective exhausting of potentially harmful fumes than to provide individual employees with respiratory protective equipment as a safeguard.

(ii) Attenuation of a noisy machine is preferable to the issue of ear defenders to all those whose hearing might be at risk as a consequence of the noise.

The principle here is one of combating risks at source rather than applying palliative measures to lessen their effect.

Adapting work to the individual

5.11 The application of ergonomic principles – adapting work to the individual, is an approach that is increasingly recognised as beneficial to individuals and their employers.

There are opportunities for ergonomic improvements in workplace design, work equipment selection/modification and production processes. The benefits from these improvements are not confined to health and safety as generally understood, but extend to the alleviation of monotony and the performance of tasks at predetermined rates.

For example display screen workstation design has improved dramatically, resulting in substantial benefits for employees required to work with display screen equipment.

Similar improvements are needed in other industries, for example in respect to the design, quality and condition of chairs provided for workers in the manufacturing and processing sectors, whose work is such that it enables them to carry it out while seated.

Applying the lessons from technological progress

5.12 It is important for employers to keep abreast of technical and technological developments related to the business they are in. These developments often result in easier and/or safer ways to do the work. In certain circumstances, for example injury or ill-health conditions, failure to apply the lessons of improved technology may be used against employers in the courts.

Coherent policy and approach to health and safety

5.13 Risk assessment is not a 'stand alone' activity. It forms part of a coherent company or organisation approach to health and safety, albeit a key part. Whether risks in the enterprise are classified as small, medium or large, the overriding objective should be to reduce *every* risk to the lowest level reasonably practicable.

5.14   Risk Assessment — Methodology

Health and Safety Policies produced in compliance with *section 2(3)* of the *Health and Safety at Work etc. Act 1974* should reinforce these principles.

Prioritise remedial measures/actions

5.14   No organisation can change everything at once. Therefore preference should be given to those measures which benefit the greatest number, i.e. by giving priority to these measures over those only providing protection to individuals.

The role of the individual

5.15   Workers and the self-employed must understand their role and responsibility for safe working, and be quite clear about what they are required to do.

Health and Safety culture

5.16   A healthy and safe workplace and work environment cannot be maintained unless there is a positive health and safety culture throughout the entire workforce. Everyone must have 'ownership' of and contribute to a positive attitude and approach to health and safety.

Controlling the risks – the process

5.17   Generally methods of controlling risks must be a matter for those directly involved in the risk assessment process. Exceptions are risks posed by particularly hazardous substances subject to regulations specifying the protective measures to be taken, for example lead and asbestos – see Chapter 8.

The following table suggests an approach which will generally take account of all the relevant factors.

Aids to effective risk control

5.18   Although it is important to consider each risk individually, and decide what action is needed to reduce each risk based upon the facts in each case, there are a number of good health and safety practice aids/requirements which, although peripheral to risk

Table 5 – Process for managing identified risks

a.	Consider the risks in strict order, i.e. high risks first.
b.	Within the high, medium and low risk classifications review each risk in descending numerical score order, i.e. risks numbered 25 first, 24 next and so on.
c.	Determine whether there are regulations in force which relate to the risk area under review – if yes the lowest standard of protection acceptable must be compliance with the regulations.
d.	In most cases, the standard of performance/compliance demanded in regulations is 'so far as is reasonably practicable'. However there are exceptions, in particular in relation to the guarding of the working parts of dangerous machines in the *Provision and Use of Work Equipment Regulations 1998*, for which the duty to protect is 'absolute'. Other regulations imposing this standard of duty include the *Control of Substances Hazardous to Health Regulations 1999* (*COSHH*) and the *Electricity at Work Regulations 1989*. Many regulations are now amplified by Approved Codes of Practice (ACOP). Unless employers are confident that their protection arrangements are as good as those called for in an ACOP, they should comply with the ACOP.
e.	If there is no regulation relevant to a risk being considered, there may still be guidance on the subject issued by the HSE, or there could be a British Standard (BS) or British Standard 'normalised' to harmonise with a standard now applicable throughout the European Union (BSEN). Finally there might be standards published by an industry or trade association or local authority, for example in respect to the issue of a licence for a single or multiple entertainment event, such as a series of concerts.
f.	Risks for which no standards as described in sub-para (e) exist should be controlled by following the 'hierarchy of measures' in paragraphs 5.8–5.12 above, in particular paragraphs 5.9 and 5.10 (Avoidance/elimination/substitution and combating risks at source).
g.	There should be adequate records of the actions agreed and arrangements for ongoing review and monitoring. Chapter 6 covers recording and documentation.
h.	Although Personal Protective Equipment (PPE) is a 'quick fix' solution to many workplace risks, it should be remembered that PPE may only be used as a last resort, i.e. when other more effective and permanent options for overcoming risks have been considered.

Notes:
Those responsible for risk assessment cannot have knowledge of all the regulations, standards etc. referred to above. This is why the involvement of the company competent safety adviser is essential.

management, can nonetheless assist in the risk management process. These include:

Table 6 – Risk assessment calculation – risks to property/plant/assets

Seriousness	Consequences	Score
Catastrophic:	complete destruction of facility	5
Major damage:	parts of operation at standstill; significant contractual failure; or total rescheduling	4
Severe damage:	significant loss of production or significant delays; or substantial costs/resources required to restore 'status quo'	3
Minor damage:	short delays in process etc; or possibility of requiring outside assistance to restore situation	2
Negligible:	capable of same-day repair or restitution by own staff and no interference with normal company operations	1

Probability/likelihood/frequency	Score
Regular occurrence	5
Frequent occurrence	4
Occasional occurrence	3
Rare occurrence	2
Remote occurrence	1

or

At least once each day	5
Three or four times a month	4
Two or three times a year	3
Once every two years	2
Unlikely to happen at all	1

(i) Safe systems of work

This term has its origins in *section 2(2)(a)* of the *Health and Safety at Work etc. Act 1974*. This section requires employers, as one of their duties in respect to the protection of their employees, to provide and maintain plant and systems of work that are safe and without risk to health.

As *section 2(2)(a)* is the first of the specific duties of employers with regard to employee health and safety, it confirms that the development of safe systems of work were viewed as pivotal when *HSWA* was drafted.

Although the Act provides no further direction in respect to safe systems of work, it is clear that for any system of work to be complied with it must be written down, certainly so if there is any degree of complexity or risk associated with it. Not to do so would invite criticism or worse in the event of a reportable accident which was subsequently investigated officially.

An inspector could hardly fail to ask the two key questions at the outset of such an investigation: 'What was the system of work being followed when the accident occurred?' and 'How much training had the injured/deceased received in that system of work?'

The existence of safe systems of work therefore, are fundamental to health and safety generally, and key in terms of risk management. However, 'safe systems of work' as envisaged by HSWA may now take different forms, and these are described.

(ii) Method statements

Method Statements and 'Permits to Work' (PTWs) (see below) are in effect safe systems of work, and represent modern versions of the 1974 requirement. Thus the term 'safe systems of work' has become a generic word, although many firms still use the original term to describe their safe systems.

Method statements are now becoming the norm across the entire spectrum of work.

They have a dual purpose; first they focus attention on the way work is to be carried out in order to confirm that it will be done safely, efficiently and to high standards; second to provide a written record of the proposed method of working which a client firm will wish to see before they permit any work to be carried out on their premises, or on their behalf.

It is becoming increasingly important for firms who employ contractors, irrespective of the reason for doing so, to require the contractors to supply method statements showing how they will carry out the work (or service) for them.

This is because client firms (employers) have a general obligation to ensure that contractors who they appoint, can do the necessary work, or provide services in a safe manner and without risks to the health of their own workforce or others. When the proposed work is of a construction nature, and falling within the ambit of the *Construction (Design and Management) Regulations 1994 (CDM)*, the client is specifically required to ensure that any contractor who he appoints is competent, and has allocated sufficient resources to carry out the work safely.

CDM applies to construction projects where the construction phase is expected to last more than 30 days or where it will involve more than 500 person days of work, for projects where there will be five or more persons working on the site at any one time, and to projects below the five person threshold if the work in question involves demolition.

5.18   Risk Assessment — Methodology

Table 7 – Minimum information – Safe System of work or Method Statement

- A risk assessment in respect to the work to be done
- Whether or not all or part of the work will be subject to compliance with a Permit to Work
- Details of physical layout and organisation for carrying out the work
- Sequence/phases of the work to be done
- Arrangements for the issue and communication of instructions
- Evidence that the staff assigned to the work are trained and competent
- Details of warnings and notices necessary to ensure safety
- Confirmation that appropriate tools and equipment will be provided
- Details to confirm that supervision will be adequate
- Details of the monitoring regime for the work

As a contractors method statement should explain how the work will be done in compliance with these objectives, this statement or statements are key,

Therefore Method Statements and/or Safe Systems of Work should explain the method of working for every stage or phase, and should contain at least the information listed in Table 7.

(iii) Permits to Work (PTW)

There are a number of common workplace operations where the potential for injury is such that special arrangements must be in place as a condition for carrying out the work.

These arrangements take the form of a 'Permit to Work' which means that the work in question cannot be undertaken unless a specific permit to allow it to do so exists.

Examples of work which should be subject to a permit to work include:

-    work in confined spaces;

-    work with high voltage electricity;

-    work in places where access is difficult and/or recovery of an injured person would be difficult;

-    pressure testing;

-    work near to or requiring the use of highly flammable, explosive or toxic substances;

-    work at heights or on roofs;

-    diving operations;

– work involving demolition of pipelines or opening of plant containing steam, ammonia, chlorine, hazardous chemicals, vapours, gases or liquids under pressure.

Requirements of Permits to work

If the permit to work system is to provide the safeguards intended, the following requirements must always be satisfied:

(1) The permit must specify clearly who is to do the work, the time for which the permit is valid, the nature of the work to be done and the precautions to be taken.

(2) During the currency of the permit, it supersedes all other instructions relevant to the work or operation in question.

(3) During the currency of the permit, no person may work at any place or on any plant not identified as safe by the permit to work.

(4) No person may carry out any work not specifically called for in the permit. If a change in the work to be done or in the sequence is required, this may only be authorised by the originator of the permit.

(5) Where the permit holder changes, for example in an emergency, the new holder must take full responsibility for the work, either until all the authorised work has been completed, or the temporary permit holder formally returns the permit to the originator.

(6) Appropriate liaison must be initiated with other work areas that could be affected by work authorised by permit.

(7) Where confusion could arise as to the geographic limits of work areas covered by a permit, the limits of these areas must be clearly indicated.

(8) Where contractors are employed, they should be aware of the requirement for permits to work where these apply, and the contractual arrangements with contractors should include a requirement to comply with a client firms permit to work arrangements.

Permits to work – cancellation

Once work subject to permit is completed, the permit should be cancelled and returned to the originator, who should ensure that the work in question has been completed satisfactorily, and that all personnel, plant and equipment have been removed from the area.

The person responsible for the plant and equipment should ensure that it has been returned to his charge, and complete the appropriate section (Part I) of the permit to work (see the end of this chapter).

Permit to work – documentation

Ideally permits should be printed in triplicate, self-carbonned and serially numbered; the originator should distribute copies as follows:

(a)   the original to the person undertaking the work. It may be appropriate to display the permit at the place of work as an additional check/safeguard;

(b)   the first copy to the person responsible for the area in which the work is to be carried out;

(c)   the second copy should be retained by the originator;

Permits to Work – summary

Permits to work are an essential safeguard where the work to be done poses significant risks. Where they are used, they constitute a 'Safe system of work'.

In terms of risk assessment, permits to work should satisfy the requirements of *regulation 3* of *MHSWR* as the permit will incorporate all the measures necessary to ensure health and safety for the duration of the work activity in question.

Chapter 6 of this handbook (Risk Assessment – Documentation) includes an example of a risk assessment where the remedial measures include compliance with a Permit to Work.

It is important to recognise that although a PTW for a specific work activity – for example working on roofs, will contain some basic requirements which will be applicable whenever work on roofs takes place, the 'standard' or generic roof working PTW must be 'customised' each time it is used for work to be carried out on roofs.

Moreover, the ongoing arrangements for risk management must include periodic review of all 'standard' permits to work to ensure that the basic safety rules they contain continue to reflect the latest thinking and developments in respect to the work operations to which they relate.

PERMIT TO WORK CERTIFICATE

LOCATION: **ORIGINATOR:**   **DATE:**

PART A
Valid from .... (time) to .... (time) on .... (date)
Issued by .... to ....
This permit is issued for the following work ....
in .... department/area/section.

PART B – PRECAUTIONS	YES/NO	N/A	SIGNATURE
1 The above plant has been removed from service and persons under my supervision have been informed.			
2 The above plant has been isolated from all sources of: (a) ingress of dangerous fumes, flammable and toxic substances (b) electrical and mechanical power; (c) heat, steam and/or hot water.			
3 The above plant has been freed of dangerous substances.			
4 Atmospheric tests have been carried out and the atmosphere is safe.			
5 The area is roped off or otherwise segregated from adjacent areas.			
6 The appropriate danger/caution notices have been displayed.			
7 The following additional safety precautions have been taken: (a) the use of safety belt and life line; (b) the use of goggles and/or gloves; (c) the use of flameproof lamps; (d) the use of fresh air/self-contained breathing apparatus; (e) prohibition on naked lights/sources of ignition; (f) .... (g) .... (h)			

Part C – DECLARATION
I hereby declare that the operations detailed in Parts A and B have been completed and that the above particulars are correct.
Signed .... Date .... Time ....

PART D – RECEIPT/ACCEPTANCE OF CERTIFICATE
I have read and understand this certificate and will undertake to work in accordance with the conditions in it.
Signed .... Date .... Time ....

PART E – COMPLETION OF WORK
The work has been completed and all persons under my supervision, materials and equipment have been withdrawn.
Signed .... Date .... Time ....

PART F – REQUEST FOR EXTENSION
The work has NOT been completed and permission to continue is requested.
Signed .... Date .... Time ....

5.18 Risk Assessment — Methodology

PART G – EXTENSION
I have re-examined the plant detailed above and confirm that the certificate may be extended to expire at .... (time).
Further precautions ....
Signed .... Date .... Time ....

PART H – CANCELLATION OF PERMIT
I hereby declare this Permit to Work cancelled and that all precautionary measures specified have been withdrawn.
Signed........................... .... Date .... Time ....

PART I – RETURN TO SERVICE
I accept the above plant back into service.
Signed .... Date .... Time ....

PART J – REMARKS, SPECIAL CONDITIONS AND EXTRA
       INFORMATION

....
....
....
....
....
....
....
....

Quick reference checklist for Chapter 5: Risk Assessment – Methodology

Requirements	Relevant paragraphs
– Is the formula for assessing risk determined, and is it understood by everyone in the organisation?	5.3
– Do those responsible for risk control follow the process described in 5.17 or a similar process?	5.17
– Where safe systems of work, method statements and/or permits to work (PTWs) form part of the risk control measures, are registers of these aids maintained and is a 'Master copy' of each held centrally in controlled conditions?	5.18
– Where any or all of the above mentioned aids to risk control are in use, is there a procedure in place calling for their review/update at the following intervals:	
(a) Routinely – at prescribed intervals;	
(b) By exception – When the risk profile for which they have been developed changes, i.e. review of the safe system etc. follows review of the risk itself?	5.18

Appendix A

Example of a risk assessment method varying the '5×5' method by increasing frequency and severity options to 6 in each case, thus allowing for values between 1 and 36.

SCORE	PROBABLE FREQUENCY
1	A highly improbable occurrence
2	A remotely possible but unknown occurrence
3	An occasional occurrence
4	A fairly frequent occurrence
5	A frequent and regular occurrence
6	Almost a certainty

SCORE	SEVERITY
1	Negligible injuries
2	Minor injuries
3	Major injuries
4	Single fatality
5	Multiple fatality
6	Multiple fatality (On & off site)

		SEVERITY				
		6	5	4	3	2	1
F R E Q U E N C Y	6	36	30	24	18	12	6
	5	30	25	20	15	10	5
	4	24	20	16	12	8	4
	3	18	15	12	9	6	3
	2	12	10	8	6	4	2
	1	6	5	4	3	2	1

Example of a risk assessment method using 4 degrees of severity/ seriousness and 6 of likelihood, with each of the degrees quantified. Note that no numerical values are assigned, determination of classification high, medium or low is already plotted according to the severity and likelihood determined.

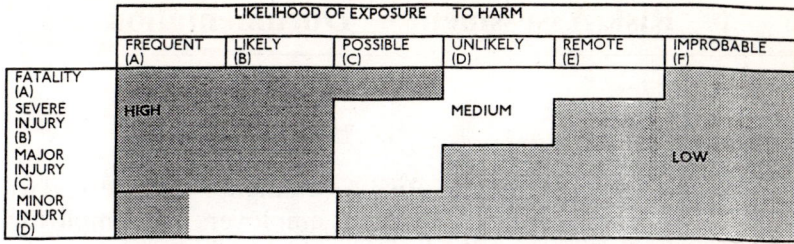

Severity

DESCRIPTION	CODE	DEFINITION
FATALITY	A	Multiple or single fatality per event
SEVERE INJURY	B	Multiple or single severe/disabling injury or occ illness per event
MAJOR INJURY	C	RIDDOR Major injury per event/injury resulting in >3 days absence from work
MINOR INJURY	D	Injury requiring medical attention and leading to absence from work not exceeding 3 days.

Likelihood

DESCRIPTION	CODE	DEFINITION
Frequent	A	Occurs at least every month
Likely	B	Occurs at least once a year
Possible	C	Occurs at least once every few years
Unlikely	D	Expected to occur during lifecycle of the structure (20–150 yrs)
Remote	E	Unlikely to occur during life-cycle of structure
Improbable	F	Extremely unlikely to occur during lifecycle of structure

6   Risk Assessment — Documentation

Introduction

6.1   *Regulation 3(4)* of *MHSWR* – Risk Assessment – is concerned with risk assessment recording; it requires employers who employ five or more employees to record the 'significant findings' of the risk assessment, and any group of their employees identified by the assessment as being especially at risk.

Regulation 8(a) of *MHSWR* – Information for Employees – requires employers to provide 'comprehensible and relevant' information to their employees about risks to their health and safety identified by the risk assessment carried out to comply with *regulation 3*, while *regulation 8(e)* calls for employers to provide their employees with details of any risks notified to them by other employers who share the same work premises or site, which could pose a threat to their health and safety.

Regulation 9(1)(c) of *MHSWR* – Co-operation and Co-ordination – requires employers who share their work premises with other employers to inform the other employers of any risks to their employees' health and safety which are posed by their own operations.

Regulations 8 and *9* are therefore complementary to *regulation 3*, in that they relate to communication of the conclusions of risk assessments to all those who need to know.

Some confusion has arisen about the term 'significant findings' in *regulation 3(4)*, given that the purpose of risk assessments is the protection of people. In the world of finance, auditors and accountants are properly vigilant about everything, however insignificant.

Benefits from recording all 'findings'

6.2   Although *regulation 3(4)* of *MHSWR* only requires significant findings to be recorded, many firms opt to record all their findings because they recognise that doing so not only completes the process in a tidy manner, but provides them with important information – and an audit trail in the sense that risk assessment work, once completed, is an important management tool. If all the conclusions from the risk assessment exercise were not recorded, particularly in larger organisations, much valuable data would be lost, and time wasted.

For example, a particular risk is evaluated and after proper consideration, applying the assessment criteria used by the company in question, this results in the risk being ranked a low risk – ergo it is not 'significant'. Some months later, the situation changes and the risk has to be re-evaluated.

If the record of the earlier considerations, including the factors and calculations that determined that the risk was 'low' had not been recorded, this could mean the assessment having to be carried out again from the beginning, and without benefit of what is likely to have been a significant amount of research and calculation. This is bad enough, but the absence of such data prevents comparison of the 'then' and 'now' status, an essential comparison in the re-evaluation exercise.

It is also important to stress the general duty of employers to reduce risks to the lowest level reasonably practicable. Because a risk is classified as 'low' this is not to say that it cannot be reduced further, or eliminated altogether. The danger in not recording low risks is that they will be forgotten.

Finally, Chapter 9 refers to the Millennium 2000 problem, and the attention which HSE Inspectors are giving to the progress or otherwise of firms in preparing themselves for the millennium.

The HSE have made clear that they will take action against any firm whose dilatoriness in planning for this event gives rise to danger. Clearly the millennium problem is very significant, and therefore must appear in risk assessments, whether or not a company has taken action, and whether on not their conclusion is that the risk is significant or otherwise. If they rank this risk as low (insignificant) and therefore do not record it on their risk assessments, they will nonetheless have to resurrect all their calculations to satisfy a visiting inspector.

Reviewing risk assessments

6.3   Risk assessment is a dynamic process, and to be effective, an assessment, once made, should be reviewed as follows:

— if law or regulation relating to the subject of the risk changes, review will be necessary to ensure that the risk mitigating measures taken achieve the standards or include the measures required by the changed law, regulation or ACOP;

6.4   Risk Assessment — Documentation

— if significant operational/production changes occur within the organisation; and

— at a predetermined frequency as a routine.

On each occasion that risk assessment review takes place a record must be made, not only to date the review, but to record the changes made, or decision not to change the 'status quo', as the case may be. If this does not happen, risk assessment records will be disjointed and uncoordinated.

Guidance on requirements for record keeping

6.4 Although there is a considerable amount of official guidance on the risk assessment process itself, information and guidance in respect to recording in *regulation 3(4)(b)* of *MHSWR* and its ACOP is confined to the following:

— employers must record the significant findings of the (risk) assessment; and

— any groups of employees identified by it as being especially at risk;

— the assessment will normally be in writing, although it may be recorded by other means, for e.g. electronically provided that the information can be retrieved readily when required for use by management or examination by those entitled to examine it, such as a statutory inspector or safety representative.

Significant findings

6.5 'Significant findings' should include:

(a) the significant hazards identified, i.e. those that might pose serious risks to workers or others who might be affected by the work activity if the hazards were not properly controlled;

(b) the existing control measures in place and the extent to which they control the risks. If these measures are procedures, safe systems of work, method statements, permits to work, etc. it will suffice to endorse the 'control measures' column of the assessment record with the unique reference number or title of the controlling procedure/s, etc. See also paragraph 6.9 comments on keeping procedures, etc. under review;

(c) the population which may be affected by the significant risks or hazards, including any groups of employees who are at special or greater risk than the main workforce.

The ACOP summarises its guidance on record keeping by stating that in many case employers (or the self-employed) will need to record sufficient detail of the assessment as to be able to demonstrate to an inspector or safety representative that they have carried out a suitable and sufficient assessment capable of being readily reviewed and amended if circumstances change.

If any the various methodologies adopted for classifying risks (see Chapter 5) had included a formula which resulted in risks being classified as 'significant' or 'insignificant' (or 'not significant'), this would have made compliance with the recording requirements of these regulations much more straightforward. As Chapter 5 shows, the alpha and/or numeric methods commonly used to classify risks usually produce risk classifications of 'High' 'Medium' or 'Low'.

Clearly a high risk is a significant risk, but does this also hold good for a medium risk? Probably it does. Fortunately in the interests of completeness, efficiency, assessment review, saving on time and resource, the majority of organisations record *all* their risk assessments findings, whether the risk is classified as high, medium or low.

Removing risks from the record

6.6 Paragraph 6.2 does not imply that a risk, having appeared on the assessment documentation must remain on it, thus causing risk assessments to expand in size indefinitely. Given the general requirement to reduce all risks to the lowest level reasonably practicable, many risks appearing on the risk assessment record will be removed over time.

For example, working in an office or factory alone after the end of normal working hours, or at weekends, clearly represents a considerable risk compared to working during normal hours, when the workers' colleagues are around and will notice if there is an accident, assault, traumatic illness, etc.

Therefore, in the circumstances described above, the risk is, to use the terminology of the regulations, 'significant'. There are a variety of measures that could be taken to mitigate the risk described. These include requiring that at least two people are present when in the workplace outwith normal hours, having a telephone check procedure, employing resident or peripatetic security guards, etc.

Each of these measures reduces the risk described to some extent, but do not overcome it altogether. However, if management decreed that no employee was permitted to work after normal hours or at week-ends, and that the keys of the premises ceased to be made available, the risk would no longer exist, and can be removed from the assessment record. Of course this would require a suitable entry on the record to explain how it has been eliminated, and the date on which the changes were made.

This is not to suggest that the remedy for all 'working alone' situations is to stop them; patently this is not possible. However, it is likely that in a great many cases, such working is tacitly condoned because it is seen to be beneficial to the enterprise and consequently management make no comment on the practice.

Unfortunately, aside from the direct health and safety implications already referred to, there may be other underlying reasons why 'out of hours' working occurs, for example an unrealistic workload, inefficiency of the worker, anxiety to please, hope of preferment and many other factors. There could also be other problems associated with the introduction of the *Working Time Regulations 1998*.

Insofar as record keeping is concerned, the measures described which fall short of stopping the practice of 'out-of-hours' working altogether mean that the risk (and the measures to ameliorate it) must remain on the record. Only if 'out-of-hours' working is banned can the risk be removed from the record.

The starting point for risk assessment recording

6.7   On the day that the duty to record the significant findings of risk assessments became law (1 January 1993), some firms already had in place arrangements, procedures or systems which so closely resembled the requirements of *regulation 3* that they needed the minimum of modification to achieve full compliance.

Others had been carrying out risk assessments and taking appropriate action to remove or mitigate the risks which they had identified, without formalising the process or knowing that the actions that they had been taking would eventually be formalised in the way that they have.

In firms having some high risk operations, management attention might have been focused upon these risks to the exclusion of all else. Consequently other risk areas within the firm were not addressed at all, in the belief that the level of risk in these areas was not such as to warrant attention, especially so when compared to the high risk operations.

Of course there were huge numbers of companies, who, given the nature of their operations and work processes, assumed that they were inherently safe, and had carried out no form of risk assessment whatever.

These firms were mostly in the commercial sector, and when evaluation of their risks was carried out usually highlighted the following areas of concern, which are listed in order of prevalence – DSE work, manual handling and working alone. The first two of these potential risk areas are discussed in Chapter 3 and working alone is referred to in paragraph 6.6 of this chapter.

The format and content of risk assessment records

6.8   It has been stated that most organisations include in their risk assessment records details of all the risk currently posed by their operations, whether such risks are categorised as 'high' 'medium' or 'low'; this means that the record will be of greater length than if it had been confined to what *regulation 3* describes as 'significant findings'.

The problem with risk records is not one of length, but of breadth. So much information is required to satisfy *regulation 3* that the information must of necessity be condensed by the use of codes, abbreviations and reference to documents containing the detail of the arrangements to eliminate or reduce the risk.

Paragraphs 6.3 and 6.4 discussed what the assessment record should cover. The following summarises these requirements:

—   the record must show the 'significant findings', i.e. the most serious of the risks assessed; they must show sufficient detail and be capable of being reviewed regularly

—   the risks must be accompanied by details of the existing control measures; and

—   indicate if any group of employees is especially at risk and whether any non-employees are also exposed.

Basic risk assessment recording

6.9   Table 1 is an example of the most basic kind of risk assessment record. For ease of explanation *only*, each column in the table has an alphabetic reference. The sole purpose of this is to make for ease of understanding/reference generally.

Notes on Table 1

Column (a) – risk reference number

This column has no relevance to the process itself, but is simply a way to make quick reference to a particular risk. In some organisations there might be dozens of risks in the schedule, hence the importance of assigning a discrete number to each risk for ease of reference. This number has no relevance to the importance of a risk. Risk number 1 for example, could be a risk ranked/rated as 'low'.

Column (b) – Description of risk

Care must be taken to ensure that the risk is identified in a way that the reader can comprehend accurately and quickly. For example, 'slippery floors' gives some information, but 'slippery floors – works canteen' is more focused.

For projects or operations which consist of a number of phases or stages, it will be necessary to present the risk information in a logical/sequential manner. For example a construction project will normally be subject to the *Construction (Design and Management) Regulations 1994 (CDM)* – see Chapter 8, paragraphs 8.46–8.55.

Such projects could be divided into a number of generic phases, including but not confined to planning, mobilisation, ground-works, structural work, fitting-out, completion, commissioning and handover. Within each of these phases, in particular structural work, there could be a number of phases.

Similarly in a production/manufacturing process there might be a number of stages in the process.

Columns (c) (d) (e) and (f)

The purpose of these columns is to indicate which categories of people are at risk – Employees, Contractors, the Public or Visitors. No guidance is provided in the regulations or ACOP guidance with regard to establishing the actual numbers at risk, therefore the applicable columns may be ticked, or ticked together with the insertion of the approximate numbers involved. Alternatively percentages can be used, for example employees 90 per cent, Contractors five per cent, public and visitors five per cent.

Table 1 – Basic/simple form of risk assessment record

| No. | Hazard Identified | Persons at risk | | | Existing Controls | Consequence category | Frequency category | Risk level |
		EMP	CON	PUB	VIS				
(A)	(B)	(C)	(D)	(E)	(F)	(G)	(H)	(I)	(J)

Frequently a risk is only posed to a small number of workers, and it is important to make this clear. Therefore it is useful to state the approximate total number of employees in a given plant or office, and then to state the number (or percentage) that are affected by the risk in question. A further refinement is to show the number or percentage, and then to indicate where in the premises those at risk work, if this information is not explicit in the risk description.

Obviously quantification, even if only approximate, puts the risk into a context.

Column (g) – Existing controls

This column is for the purpose of explaining what the current situation is with regard to controlling the risk. As explained in Chapter 5, many if not most of the controlling measures will be written down as a procedure, etc. and if each procedure has a discrete reference, inserting the title and reference number is sufficient.

The term 'procedure' is generic in this context, and covers a number of forms of record; many have titles in common usage, others are meaningful only to the company using them. Examples in common use are safe systems of work, safe operating systems, standard operating procedures, method statements and permits to work (PTWs).

It is recommended that the Risk Assessment Group or a person appointed by them maintains a 'master copy' of the company risk assessment, together with copies of all the written procedures, etc. which are referred to in the controlling measures column of the risk assessment.

If copies of these procedures are not kept with the master copy of the risk assessment record, this will waste time and create a poor impression in the event that a statutory inspector wished to review the risk assessment. Once a procedure or system, etc. is referred to in the risk assessment record, that system has effectively become a part of the assessment record, so a copy should be kept with the 'master copy' of the risk assessment.

Columns (h) (i) and (j)

These columns shown the calculation and final risk category determined applying the calculation method adopted by the business or organisation. If the method used follows the 5×5 principal (see Chapter 5), it is useful, particularly for subsequent reference, to show how the final calculation of risk score was arrived at. Therefore in columns (h) and (i) there will be a figure between 1 and 5, with a total figure not exceeding 25 in column (j), beside which will be the final ranking of the risk – high, medium, or low.

If risk assessment is carried out using a basic intuitive method, i.e. on a show of hands agreeing whether the risk is low (L), medium (M) or high (H) (see Chapter 5), then columns (h) and (i) are not used, and only column (j) used to show whether the risk is ranked (L) (M) or (H).

General comment

6.10   As stated at the beginning of paragraph 6.9 Table 1 is an example of the most basic approach to risk assessment recording.

It shows a calculation of the status of a given risk at the time the assessment was carried out. There is no record of the previous 'history' of the risk, nor any indication whether any further measures are possible or planned. The premise here is that the risk has been ranked taking account of the control measures described, ie the risk with control measures in place. It does not show what the risk ranking would have been without the control measures.

Although most firms would consider this approach as lacking in detail, and not providing sufficient information for their ongoing arrangements for the management of risks, it would probably be acceptable for the purpose of complying with *regulation 3*.

However, Table 2 which follows, shows that with relatively little additional effort much more meaningful information can be provided.

Notes on Table 2

Columns (a) to (f) inclusive – same as Table 1

Columns (g), (h) and (i) correspond to (h), (i) and (j) in Table 1, but the 'Existing Controls' column as in Table 1 now becomes column (j) and is followed by a new column (k) titled 'Revised risk'.

Effectively this moves the 'existing controls' column to a position *after* the first calculation of risk value, and then adds an entirely new column at the end – 'revised risk'. The rationale for this follows.

6.10 Risk Assessment — Documentation

Table 2 – Improved form of risk assessment record

No.	Hazard Identified	Persons at risk				Consequence Category	Frequency Category	Risk Level	Existing Controls	Revised Risk
		EMP	CON	PUB	VIS					
(A)	(B)	(C)	(D)	(E)	(F)	(G)	(H)	(I)	(J)	(K)

Experience with risk assessment recording has highlighted the fact that there should be a calculation of each risk in its 'raw' form, i.e. without the implementation of *any mitigating measures*

The 'added value' of this approach is that *all* the measures that the employer has taken to mitigate the risk in question appear on the record, even if these measures were taken earlier – perhaps even before the introduction of *MHSWR* and *regulation 3*. This is important, not only from a company record standpoint, but also to show the extent to which employers have addressed particular risks over time.

Thus Table 2 improves upon Table 1 by showing two risk ratings, the first the risk in its natural uncontrolled form, the second its new (reduced) rating as a consequence of the mitigating (or controlling or management) measures introduced by the employer since the risk first arose in connection with the conduct of the employers business.

It will be noted that column (k) – revised risk, is not preceded by columns equivalent to the 'consequence' and 'frequency' columns (g) and (h) which precede 'risk level' – column (i). This is not an omission but an endeavour to get all the information in. Therefore the calculation to arrive at the revised risk – column (k) still has to be made as for columns (g), (h) and (i).

Ideally the constituent figures should be shown and the final numerical value and its interpreted 'revised risk level' – low, medium or high inserted.

Further improvements are possible. Table 2 still only provides a snapshot of the situation at the time of examination or review of a company risk profile. It makes no provision for recording any further improvements that are possible or necessary, for example if the level of risk is considered to be too high or unacceptable.

Review of risk assessment

6.11 Paragraph 6.2 described the circumstances which should bring about the review of an existing risk assessment, i.e. when law changes make it necessary, when a company's operations significantly change, and routinely.

In this respect *regulation 4* of *MHSWR* (Health and Safety Arrangements) has a bearing. *Regulation 4* requires every employer to make and give effect to such arrangements as are appropriate, having regard to the size and nature of the organization, for effectively planning, organising, controlling, *monitoring and reviewing* the measures taken by him to prevent and protect against risks to health and safety, and if he has five or more employees, to record these arrangements.

Given the status of risk assessment in the health and safety equation, the requirement to monitor and review the risk assessment must be paramount in terms of complying with *regulation 4*.

The risk assessment record tables numbered 1 and 2 therefore both need to include provisions to record details of subsequent reviews – whether carried out routinely, or due to changes in law and regulation or the employers operations. These details include the date of the review, any further actions deemed necessary, dates for completion of action required, and assignment of responsibility for implementation.

Although the suggested review details have not been appended to Tables 1 and 2, they do appear in the sample risk assessment Table 3.

Table 3 – sample risk assessment

6.12 In order to have relevance to the widest range of work sectors, the risks appearing in this table are diverse and not typical of any one industry sector.

Notes on Table 3

Risk 3A – Working alone outwith normal hours – column (M) refers to Safe Working Practice No 123. This is for illustration purposes only.

However, a safe working practice in relation to working alone should include, but not be limited to, some or all of the following:

(i)   —   No member of staff (or employee) to work after 1800 hours week-days, or at week-ends or on Bank Holidays without the prior written authorisation of their manager, using Form 01.

—   A copy of Form 01 must be passed to Security by 1600 hours of the day when late working is to take place (week-days), or, in respect to weekend working, by 1600 hours on the Friday beforehand. Arrangements in respect to Bank Holidays will be advised two working weeks before the holiday.

Numerical values
Score: 16–25 = high risk
9–15 = medium risk
<9 = low risk

Table 3 – Model risk assessment

J Smith Ltd Location Office and Warehouse, Anytown (500 employees)

A	B	C	D	E	F		G	H	I	J	K	L	M
No	Hazard Identified	Persons at Risk					Cons. Cate-gory	Freq. Cate-gory	Risk level	Existing Controls	Revised Risk	Date of Review	Revised Risk
		EMP	CON	PUB	VIS								
1	Risks associated with working with DSE	45	–	–	–		–>	–>	–>	See separate DSE assessments		N/A	
2	Health risks associated with MHO	50	–	–	–		–>	–>	–>	See separate Manual Handling Assessments		N/A	
3	Working alone or in isolation, as follows:												
3A	Working alone after 1800 hrs Mon-Fri at weekends or bank hols	5% of staff	–	–	–		4	2	8	None	8	See Safe Working Practice No 123 - Working Alone	6 (3x2)
3B	Working normal hours but in isolation	4% of staff	–	–	–		5	4	20	Issued with 2-way radios	12 (4x3)	See Safe Working Practice No 124 - Working in Isolation	6 (3x2)

Table 3 – **Model risk assessment** *(continued)*

A	B	Persons at Risk				G	H	I	J	K	L	M
No	Hazard Identified	EMP	CON	PUB	VIS	Cons. Category	Freq. Category	Risk level	Existing Controls	Revised Risk	Date of Review	Revised Risk
4	FLT – Collision with Pedestrians	All	5	–	–	4	3	12	FLT Drivers Certificated FLT fitted with horns/strobe lights	15 (5x3)	Demarcation of Pedestrian routes & crossing points. Erection of barriers. Training/induction of all staff using/ required to walk through warehouse	
5	Improper entry to premises	All	5	–	–	4	3	12	Visual check by security at main gate	12 (4x3)	Visitors to sign in, wear ID, to be met at reception, be accompanied at all times and escorted to reception at departure	4 (4x1)
6	Fire risk assessment											
6:1	Obstruction of Fire Exit area outside rear office door (emergency exit) by parked vehicles	50	Y	–	Y	5	2	10	None	10	(a) Affix sign on outwards facing side of door: 'Fire Exit – Do Not Obstruct'	

Table 3 – Model risk assessment (*continued*)

A	B	C	D	E	F	G	H	I	J	K	L	M
No	Hazard Identified	Persons at Risk				Cons. Cate-gory	Freq. Cate-gory	Risk level	Existing Controls	Revised Risk	Date of Review	Revised Risk
		EMP	CON	PUB	VIS							
											(b) Paint ground with hatching (c) Day Security to check area twice per day to ensure clear of vehicles. If not, discipline employees. Purchasing to deal with suppliers and deliveries	5 (5x1)
6:2	Propping open external fire doors	50	2	–	–	5	2	10	Wrong coloured notices on doors 'Fire Doors Keep Shut'	10	(a) Replace wrong col-oured notices (b) Remove door wedges (c) Warn staff by notices/meeting (d) Initiate feas-ibility study re: electronic doors	5 (5x1)

153

Table 3 – Model risk assessment *(continued)*

A	B	C	D	E	F	G	H	I	J	K	L	M
No	Hazard Identified	Persons at Risk				Cons. Category	Freq. Category	Risk level	Existing Controls	Revised Risk	Date of Review	Revised Risk
		EMP	CON	PUB	VIS							
6:3	Inaudible fire alarm	20	2	–	–	5	2	2	Fire alarm bell test every Monday at 11 am	5 (5x1)	(a) Post notices on H&S boards advising staff to report inaudible fire alarm (b) Include (a) in company H&S policy (c) remind staff and visitors (via notices) of alarm test on the day (Although a number of extra measures have been made to make the test more effective, such measures cannot alter the consequences of alarm failure, so there is no lower risk rating in column K)	5 (5x1)

154

(ii)   There must be minimum of two persons present whenever work takes place after 1800 hours week-days, at week ends or on Bank Holidays. Persons intending to work at these times should contact ... to discuss 'Pairing'.

(iii) Security are required to make hourly checks on the well-being of staff authorised to work outwith normal hours.

(iv) All staff authorised to work outside normal hours are required to sign in/out as follows:

—   weekends/bank holidays – sign in and out

—   Monday-Friday evenings – sign out only

(v)   Security to report all instances where unauthorised out-of-hours working has taken place.

- In cases where the business does not employ a security officer or security contractor, the procedure would be quite different; for example there would be a requirement to provide details of the home telephone number of a company duty manager or equivalent, who staff working outwith normal hours would have to telephone at hourly intervals and before leaving the premises. The duty manager would then have to take appropriate action in the event that a lone worker did not report in.

   There are a number of possible permutations of the above, for example telephone checks arranged with a firm specialising in this kind of telephone surveillance. Other options are to invest in a computer based telephone check-back system.

NB: The above requirements relate to health and safety considerations only. There would also be some other administrative/remuneration matters for inclusion in this procedure.

Risk 3B – Working in isolation during normal hours – column (M) refers to Safe Working Practice No 124. This is for illustration purposes only. However, a procedure to deal with the health and safety of staff working in isolation during normal hours should include, but not be limited to, the following:

(i)   No employee is permitted to work alone in the following circumstances:

—   work with dangerous tools and equipment, mobile ladders and platforms;

—   working at heights or in confined spaces;

—   hot work;

—   work over or on water;

—   work with HV electricity;

—   in any other circumstances which the company may from time to time determine.

(ii)   Employees must inform their supervisor before commencing and on completion of, work which keeps them in isolation from colleagues.

(iii) When working in isolation, employees should carry a 2-way telephone.

(iv) If the work is expected to last more than 30 minutes, the lone worker must telephone their supervisor every 30 minutes.

(v)   The lone workers supervisor is responsible for monitoring receipt of calls from subordinates who are working in isolation, and taking action in the event of their failure to report in.

NB: items (iii)–(v) assume that 2-way telephones, or other hand-held communication tools are issued. If they are not, and cannot be justified, alternative safeguards must be incorporated into the procedure.

Summary

6.13 This chapter on risk assessment recording emphasises that the compilation and maintenance of accurate and up-to-date records is crucial to the effectiveness of risk management. Chapter 4 – Risk Assessment Preparation – discussed the various information sources that can assist those responsible for risk assessment.

Although the assessment record cannot be available prior to the first exercise aimed at developing a risk assessment, it must be a key tool at the hand of those responsible for ongoing review/ update of a firm's risk assessment record called for by *regulation 4* of *MHSWR*.

However, this tool cannot be effective unless the record reflects the current status; nothing can do more to jeopardise the effectiveness of the risk assessment effort overall than that the records of what has been achieved are out of date.

Quick reference checklist for Chapter 6: Risk Assessment – Documentation

Requirements	Relevant Paragraphs
— Has a decision been taken on the question of including all risks assessed on the risk assessment forms (whether classified as high, or low), or only those classified as medium or high?	6.2
— Do your procedures for compliance with *regulation 3* of *MHSWR* stipulate the circumstances/frequency of review of the risk assessment?	6.3
— When a risk is removed from the risk assessment record as a result of it being eliminated, is a suitable record kept of this fact?	6.6
— Has the method of recording risks been agreed and do all those responsible for recording details understand and follow the agreed format?	6.7 to 6.10 and associated tables

7 Risk Assessment Requirements for Special Categories of Worker

7.1 Every employer will at some time employ young persons, people with disabilities and women of child-bearing age. When they do so, it is important that they take account of legislation enacted to protect such people, in particular that calling for special risk assessments.

Legislation concerned with the employment of persons in each of these groups has a common thread – the requirement to assess the risks associated with the work tasks which they are or will be expected to perform, posed either by their youth, disability or pregnant condition. The specific risk assessment requirements are different in each case, and each is discussed.

Children and Young Persons

Risk assessment requirements clarified

7.2 When the requirement to undertake risk assessments first appeared in the *Management of Health and Safety at Work Regulations* in 1992, (calling for risk assessments to be in place by 1 January 1993), there was no expressed requirement to differentiate between risks to employees generally, and those to children and young persons in particular.

As a consequence of the introduction of the *Health and Safety (Young Persons) Regulations 1997, regulation 3* of *MHSWR* was amended to require risk assessments to consider risks to which children and young persons might be exposed in the event they were employed.

A child is a person below the compulsory school-leaving age, i.e. 16 years. A young person is a person over 16 years but not yet 18 years of age.

Special risk assessment required for young people

7.3 Before a child or young person commences work, a risk assessment must be undertaken and, in the case of a child, the parents of the child (or those *in loco parentis*), as well as the prospective employee must be provided with a copy.

The risk assessment should contain details of risks to the health and safety of the child while at work, and the measures taken to eliminate, mitigate and control the risks.

The Children (Protection at Work) Regulations 1998

7.4   The *Children (Protection at Work) Regulations 1998* have introduced further restrictions on child employment, which together with earlier legislation, prohibit the employment of children in the following circumstances:

(a)   where the child is under 13 years of age;

(b)   where the work is other than light work;

(c)   before the end of school hours on a school day;

(d)   for more than two hours on any school day;

(e)   before 0700 or after 1900 on any day;

(f)   for more than two hours on any Sunday;

(g)   for more than eight hours (or five hours if under 15) on any day on which they are not required to attend school and which is not a Sunday;

(h)   for more than 35 hours (25 hours if under 15) in any week during which they are not required to attend school;

(i)   for more than four hours in any day without a rest break of one hour;

(j)   at any time in a year when children are on holiday unless they have had at least two consecutive weeks without employment (i.e. they are on holiday).

Role of local authorities

7.5   Responsibility for the implementation of regulations and development of bye-laws in relation to the employment of children rests with local authorities, and it is likely that most local authorities will maintain a list of 'permitted occupations' for 13 year olds, and stipulate that a child may not work for the entire period of the main school holidays.

Work deemed unsuitable for young people

7.6   (1)   Physical agents:

(a)   work with potential exposure to ionizing radiations;

(b)   work in a high-pressure atmosphere, e.g. pressurised containers, diving.

(2)   Specified biological agents.

(3)   Chemical agents classified as being toxic, very toxic corrosive or explosive; or

(a)   substances deemed harmful or irritant carrying one or more of the following risks:

— irreversible effects;

— sensitisation by inhalation and/or skin contact;

— carcinogens;

— heritable generic damage;

— infertility or harm to unborn child;

(b)   lead or lead compounds absorbable by human contract;

(c)   asbestos.

(4)   Manufacturing and handling fireworks or explosives.

(5)   Work with fierce or poisonous animals.

(6)   Industrial scale animal slaughter.

(7)   Work with or involving the following:

— compressed, liquefied or dissolved gases;

— vats, tanks, reservoirs or carboys containing chemical agents;

— risk of structural collapse;

— high-voltage electrical hazard;

— pacing by machinery and paid by results.

Additional considerations

7.7   In addition to the above, employers should also take the following factors into account when developing risk assessments relating to the work of children and young people:

(i)   the inexperience, lack of awareness of risks and immaturity of young persons;

(ii)   the layout and fitting-out of the workplace and workstation;

(iii) the nature, degree and duration of exposure to physical, biological and chemical agents;

(iv)   the form, range and use of work equipment and the way in which it is handled;

(v)   the organisation of processes and activities:

(vi)   the extent and quality of health and safety training provided or planned;

(vii) risks from agents, processes and work listed in paragraph 7.5;

(viii) the influence and example of older more experienced work colleagues;

(ix)   work which may be beyond the physical or psychological capacity of the young person;

(x)   work which involves a risk of accidents which young people may not recognise due to insufficient experience or training or due to paying insufficient attention to training;

(xi)   work involving a risk to health due to extremes of temperature (heat or cold), noise or vibration.

There are a number of other occupations/industries where restrictions are placed on the employment of young people. These include agriculture, where the principal prohibitions relate to riding on tractors and other farm/agricultural machinery, work offshore and certain work in the pottery industry.

Medical fitness

7.8   Where the risk assessment specifies a need, young people may be required to undergo regular medical assessments. Where employment is to be offered in a factory, the local careers office must be informed in order that where appropriate some selective medical surveillance may be initiated.

Exemptions

7.9   Risk assessments are not required where young people are engaged in occasional or part-time work involving domestic service in a private household; or work regarded as not being harmful, damaging or dangerous to young people in a family undertaking. Bye-laws may withhold exemption from the duty to develop risk assessments where children work in family businesses, if the workforce includes persons who are not close family members.

Summary

7.10 Given the number of conditions governing the employment of children and young people, the role and purpose of the risk assessment as a measure to ensure that risks to this category of employee are eliminated or reduced to the lowest level reasonably practicable is pivotal.

When preparing to carry out such assessments, paragraphs 7.4, 7.6 and 7.7 of this chapter provide a useful check-list, and the local authority bye-laws on this subject (see paragraph 7.5) will also be an important reference point.

In effect, the various requirements and prohibitions described in this chapter serve as a filter, and compliance with them is effectively a risk assessment in itself.

However, an employer proposing to employ children or young people and who has satisfied all the requirements in this chapter – and any different/additional requirements contained in the relevant bye-laws of their local authority, should still subject the work processes that the children or young people are expected to perform to the regular test of absence of risk that is contained in this handbook.

Cases

7.11 Asbestos is included in the schedule of work which is deemed unsuitable for young people – see paragraph 7.6(3)(c).

On 16 April 1999 two brothers appeared at Leeds Crown Court and were convicted of charges relating to the employment of a 14 year old and two 15 year old boys to strip out asbestos from a Birmingham factory in 1996. The work was unlicensed and resulted in the release into the environment of lethal asbestos dust. Further charges relating to work with asbestos have yet to be heard.

Commenting on the above case, the judge said 'This was an act of the most astonishing criminal responsibility. You understood the nature of asbestos and yet you distributed it around Birmingham in places where people, including children, had easy access to it'

Although no specific charges in respect to failure to carry out a suitable and sufficient risk assessment were not brought in this case, it is clear that no such assessment was made.

Pregnant Women

Statutory requirements

7.12 As with children and young people, the principal legislation relating to risk assessment (*regulation 3, MHSWR 1992*) did not specifically identify pregnant women or women of child-bearing age as requiring special attention in the development of risk assessments.

The position was changed with the introduction of the *Management of Health and Safety at Work (Amendment) Regulations 1994*, introduced to ratify the European Directive on Pregnant Workers. The effect of this amendment to *MHSWR* was to add new regulations – 13A–13C – 'Risks to new or expectant mothers'.

This regulation calls for the an assessment of the specific risks posed to the health and safety of new or expectant mothers at work, and the introduction of measures to avoid or mitigate the risks identified. The focus should not be confined to risk to the pregnant employee, but should include risks to the unborn child or the child of an employee who is breastfeeding.

The term 'new or expectant mothers' means a worker who is pregnant, has given birth within the previous six months, or who is breastfeeding. 'Given birth' means having delivered a living child or, after 24 weeks of pregnancy, a stillborn child.

Prohibited work activities

7.13 On 1 April 1998 the *Control of Lead at Work Regulations 1998* came into force. These regulations consolidated all the lead related processes which women of reproductive capacity were not to be engaged in.

These are:

(a)   In the lead smelting and refining process:

   (i)   handling, treating, sintering, smelting or refining any material containing five per cent or more of lead; or

(ii)   cleaning where any of the above activities have taken place.

(b)   In the lead acid manufacturing process:

(i)   manipulating lead oxides;

(ii)   mixing or pasting;

(iii)   melting or casting;

(iv)   trimming, cutting or abraiding of pastel plates; or

(v)   cleaning where any of the above activities have taken place.

NB: The restriction upon women of reproductive age engaging in any of the above processes is also applicable to young people.

Known risks to new and expectant mothers

7.14   The principal risks to be avoided are:

(a)   Physical agents

—   regular exposure to shocks, low-frequency vibration or excessive movement;

—   manual handling of loads where there is a risk of injury;

—   prolonged exposure to loud noise;

—   significant exposure to ionising radiation or non-ionising electromagnetic radiation;

—   extremes of heat and cold;

—   movements and postures, travelling, mental and physical fatigue and other physical burdens connected with work;

(In this respect pregnant workers may experience problems if working at heights, in tight spaces or at workstations not capable of adjusting to the increased abdominal size, especially in the later stages of pregnancy. These problems could lead to strain or sprain injuries. Dexterity, agility, co-ordination, speed of movement, reach and balance may also be affected and any one or combination of these problems could cause an accident.)

— work in hyperbaric atmospheres.

(b) Biological agents

— including listeria, rubella and chicken pox virus, tox-oplasma, cytomegalovirus, hepatitis B and HIV.

(c) Chemical agents

— a range of chemical agents known to endanger the health of pregnant women and unborn children. These include substances labelled under the *Chemicals (Hazard Information and Packaging for Supply) Regulations 1994* (*CHIP* as amended) as posing specific risks. These include:

'R40' – possible risk of irreversible effects;
'R45' – may cause cancer;
'R46' – may cause heritable generic damage;
'R61' – may cause harm to the unborn child;
'R63' – possible risk of harm to the unborn child;
'R64' – may cause harm to breastfed babies.

— chemical and industrial processes listed in *Schedule 1* – the carcinogens schedule of the *COSHH regulations*;

— mercury and mercury derivatives;

— antimiotic (cytoxic) drugs;

— known dangerous chemicals that can be absorbed through the skin, including some pesticides;

— carbon monoxide; and

— lead and lead derivatives – see paragraph 7.13;

(d) Working conditions

— including mining and work with display screen equipment (VDUs).

Action on identifying a risk

7.15 Where, following an assessment, a risk is identified, the employee concerned should be informed of the risk and the preventative measures being taken. The risk should be kept under review. In effect this requirement is no different from an employers general risk to acquaint employees with details of the 'general' risk assessment.

If it is not possible to remove/eliminate the risk, the following hierarchy of measures must be followed:

(i)   temporarily adjust the working conditions or hours of work of the exposed employee. If it is not reasonable or practical to do this, or it would not avoid the risk; then

(ii)   offer suitable alternative work. If neither of the above are viable;

(iii) suspend the employee on full pay for so long as is necessary to protect the health of the employee or that of her child.

Night work

7.16   Where a new or expectant mother does night work, and her general practitioner, works medical officer or a registered midwife issues a certificate stating that the night work would affect her health and safety, employers must first offer suitable alternative daytime work and only suspend on full pay if this cannot be found.

Other considerations

7.17   When considering the work being undertaken by a pregnant employee, and whether that work poses risks due to their condition, factors such as the possibility of morning sickness and varicose veins must be considered.

Summary

7.18   Risk assessment in relation to pregnant employees, like that for children and young people, has the benefit of published guidance and some specific restrictions; this can be found in paragraphs 7.13, 7.14, 7.16 and 7.17. Paragraph 7.19 gives details of two decisions related to risk assessments in respect to pregnant employees, one by an Industrial Tribunal, the other by an Employment Appeal Tribunal (EAT). Industrial Tribunals and Industrial Appeal Tribunals have been renamed Employment Tribunals (ET) and Employment Appeal Tribunals (EAT) respectively.

Case 1 *Hickey v Lucas Services UK Limited*

7.19   Michelle Hickey worked as a delivery driver for Lucas Services UK Ltd, who supply and distribute spare parts to the automotive industry; they employed approximately 1000 staff in 60 locations. Michelle Hickey started work for Lucas Services in February 1995 and was based in Bristol.

In April 1996, Ms Hickey discovered that she was pregnant and informed her manager. As a result of her pregnancy, she suffered a severe form of sickness (hyperemesis gravidarum) which causes dehydration and weight loss. Ms Hickey had suffered from this condition during a previous pregnancy and also from past mis-carriages.

At about the time Hickey discovered that she was pregnant, although for reasons unconnected with the pregnancy, her employers became unhappy with her performance as a driver, and following a disciplinary hearing on 11 June 1996, was given a written warning and told to transfer to work as a stores assistant in the warehouse from the following day.

Hickey was concerned about the effect that working in the ware-house would have upon her pregnancy, since the work would involved constant lifting, some of it of including batteries which weighed up to 20 lbs.

Consequently, and before taking up her new duties, Hickey saw her doctor, who advised her that because of her condition, heavy manual handling would cause vomiting, which put at risk her own health and that of the unborn child. Accordingly she was supplied with fortnightly medical certificates to cover from 12 June to 14 October 1996. These were submitted to her employer.

At the same time Hickey notified the company of her concern with regard to the risks associated with the warehouse job. Her employ-ers response was to say that it had carried out a risk assessment, but did not provide her with a copy.

The facts were that no risk assessment in relation to the warehouse job, or indeed Hickey's former driving job,were carried out until August 1996, and even these were 'general risk assessments' which did not address the specific risks in either job that would be posed if they were carried out by new and expectant mothers. The employer was unaware of HSE Guidance on risk assessment for new and expectant mothers.

Lucas's response to Hickey's concerns was to tell her to 'exercise common sense', take responsibility for her own actions and not to undertake tasks which she considered were 'inappropriate'. They did however undertake to find Hickey work which would be more appropriate to her condition, and offered her clerical work, which she carried out until going on maternity leave.

Hickey only received sick pay during her period of absence from work, which was less than her usual earnings. As a consequence that level of income was too low to reach the qualifying threshold for statutory maternity pay when she went on maternity leave. Hickey complained to an Industrial Tribunal who ruled in her favour.

It was held that because her employer knew of Ms Hickey's pregnancy, yet transferred her to work which was of a nature that would pose a risk to her and her unborn child, this had effectively suspended her from work on maternity grounds, although without full pay as is required by the Employment Rights Act 1996 (ERA).

The Tribunal noted the following:

— The employer had not asked for clarification of Ms Hickey's condition from her doctor, in particular as regards the nature of her pregnancy-related sickness and how it might be affected by her new job, even though she had informed the company of her concerns shortly after she was transferred to the stores job.

— As the company had not carried out a risk assessment, it had no way of recognising the significance of their employees concerns.

— Rather than informing itself of the risks and taking appropriate action, the company had simply told their employee that she was responsible for her own health and safety.

This is an important case in that it was probably the first Tribunal decision on a matter relating to the application of the maternity suspension provision.

From a practical standpoint it emphasises the importance of addressing the special risks that can arise when aspects of a firms operations or processes may be carried out by pregnant women and new and breastfeeding mothers, and also demonstrates that employers cannot avoid their obligations by doing nothing.

The ITs interpretation of the meaning of 'suspension' means that where an employer has failed to address the risks, an employee is entitled to take time off work and be treated as suspended within the context of *regulation 13* of *MHSWR*, if she has reasonable concerns for her health and safety, or that of the unborn child, in continuing to work in a potentially unsafe environment.

Case 2 *Day v T Pickles Farms Limited (EAT)*

7.20   Mrs Day had worked from January 1996 as a counter assistant at a sandwich shop run by her employer, Pickles Farms Ltd. She became pregnant, suffered from severe morning sickness, and found that the smell of food made her nauseous.

In November 1996 she was certified unfit for work and received statutory sick pay (SSP) until April 1997. In July 1997 she claimed unfair constructive dismissal. Her employer had failed to pay her for attending ante-natal appointments and had not carried out a risk assessment. Mrs Day claimed that had they done so, this would have resulted in her being suspended on full pay for the term of her pregnancy — *regulation 13A(3)* of *MHSWR*. Had they done this, Mrs Day would have been entitled to statutory maternity pay.

In their hearing on 12 January 1998, an industrial tribunal awarded Mrs Day damages for the loss of pay while attending ante-natal appointments, but did not agree that she had been unfairly constructively dismissed, because she had failed to inform her employer 'unequivocally' that she considered her employment to have been terminated. Mrs Day appealed to an Employment Appeal Tribunal who concurred with the ET conclusion about constructive dismissal.

The EAT concluded that there had been a failure to carry out a risk assessment specific to pregnant women under *regulations 3* and *13* of *MHSWR*. In the absence of such an assessment, the EAT had to consider what the likely outcome would have been. They concluded that there was 'at least a prospect' that working conditions might have been improved as a result of a proper risk assessment.

The employers argued that they had no duty to take any action until Mrs Day notified them in writing of her pregnancy, but the EAT found that it was a matter of common sense rather than technical burden of proof whether the pregnancy had been notified.

The appeal was allowed in part, and the question of whether or not Mrs Day had been prejudiced by the absence of a specific risk assessment was referred back to the IT for consideration.

The important message from this case is the decision of the Employment Appeal Tribunal that an employer should not wait for written notification of an employee's pregnancy before carrying out an assessment, and that its failure to carry out such an assessment could have put the employee at detriment within the provisions of the *Sex Discrimination Act 1975*.

Disabled Persons

Statutory requirements

7.21 The general requirement for employers to look after the health, safety and welfare of all their employees in *HSWA 1974*, and to carry out risk assessments and take account of the capabilities of an individual when assigning work tasks to them in *MHSWR 1992*, are amplified in respect to the disabled by the *Disability Discrimination Act 1995*. This Act requires employers to treat disabled persons equally with non-disabled persons in all matters relating to employment. The 1995 Act applies to all employers with 20 or more employees.

When it is intended to employ a person who is disabled, employers will need to develop special risk assessments relating to the risks to these employees while at work.

Where necessary employers must make reasonable changes to premises, layout of work, hours of work, etc. that might be necessary to accommodate disabled employees, providing that these changes do not infringe health and safety law.

Disability is defined in the 1975 Act as any physical, mental or sensory impairment that affects the disabled persons ability to perform normal day to day activities. The disability must also be substantial and last – or be expected to last – at least twelve months. Disability includes severe disfigurements and progressive conditions such as multiple sclerosis, AIDS, etc.

Measures to enhance safety for the disabled

7.22 Measures to permit safe use of work premises for the disabled are of two kinds – some general measures which are universally applicable, for example means of access, toilet facilities, etc. and special measures which will depend upon the nature of disability of the employee or prospective employee.

(i) Access

Ideally the following provisions should be made:

— grippable handrails (to a height of 900 mm above the surface of a ramp or the pitch line of flight of steps and 1,000 mm above the surface of a landing);

— stairs with neither sharply tapered treads nor open risers;

— wheelchair stairlifts (as an alternative to passenger lifts);

— platform lifts (as an alternative to a ramp) to enable wheelchair users to move to different levels within a storey;

— sanitary conveniences located so that a wheelchair user does not have to travel more than one storey to reach a suitable WC (i.e. one which is wheelchair manoeuvrable); for ambulant disabled people, at least one disabled WC compartment should be provided within each range of WCs in storeys not designed to be accessible to the disabled.

(ii) Other considerations

— location of lift lobby call buttons and internal lift car floor call buttons that are accessible, and if necessary with buttons superimposed with Braille numbers;

— emergency evacuation – ideally disabled employees, in particular those with mobility impairment, should be located at ground level. If this is not possible, colleagues should be assigned responsibility for the evacuation of disabled staff in an emergency. Special procedures must be developed to ensure that sufficient 'cover' exists for this contingency at all times that the disabled employee is present. Where 2-stage fire alarm systems exist, it is often the practice for nominated colleagues to evacuate a disabled employee using the lift before the second (evacuate) stage signal is given, in order not to breach the rule that lifts must not be used in a fire emergency;

— if the fire alarm system is single stage only, the provision of purpose designed chairs capable of getting the mobility impaired down staircases safely – these also require the co-operation of colleagues;

— where hearing impaired staff are present, the installation of visual warnings that the fire alarm has sounded;

— possible modification of some vending machines;

— workstation and equipment modifications, e.g. for telephones.

Implications for risk assessments

7.23 Risk assessment in relation to disabled staff is not as much of a problem as it may seem. Ideally, when a disabled person is offered employment, a meeting should be arranged in order to assess what measures/modifications are needed to ensure that the employee is not at greater risk when at work than their non-disabled colleagues.

As such measures must be *in situ* before the employee commences work, this meeting should take place in sufficient time to implement any changes needed. Access and toilet requirements should already be in place in order to comply with the 1995 Act, but refinements of these, especially so in respect to the disabled toilet fittings, might be necessary.

Quick reference checklist for Chapter 7: Risk Assessment Requirements for Special Categories of Worker

Requirements	Relevant Paragraphs
— Where children and/or young people are, or are expected to be employed, do procedures exist to ensure that special risk assessments are carried out, taking account of restrictions on certain types of work, and in relation to hours of work, providing copies of the assessment to the parents of children, etc?	7.2–7.7
— Similarly, is there a model risk assessment in existence covering every work task which might be carried out by employees who are pregnant, have given birth and/or are breast feeding? (NB: this is question is repeated in the checklist to Chapter 9. Question not applicable unless women of child bearing are or are likely to be employed)	7.12–7.14
— In addition to the general provision for the disabled in workplaces necessary to comply with the *Disabled Discrimination Act 1995*, do arrangements exist, if disabled person are likely to be employed, to discuss with them any special aids necessary, and to provide these aids before employment commences?	7.20–7.21

8   Statutory Requirements — Part 3

Introduction and scope of this chapter

8.1   Chapter 2 was devoted to the principal legislation calling for risk assessments (*MHSWR*) and Chapter 3 covered two other regulations which contain specific direction about the way in which the risk assessments, pertaining to the subject of the respective regulations were to be carried out, i.e. work with display screen equipment and manual handling respectively.

This chapter discusses other regulations calling for risk assessment, but which do not specify the *modus operandi* for developing them.

Although the general principles of risk assessment described in *regulation 3* of *MHSWR* apply to assessments carried out to comply with the regulations covered in this chapter, it is important to understand the purpose of the various assessment requirements of these regulations and the differences between them.

Personal protective equipment (PPE)

The personal protective equipment at work regulations 1992 (PPE)

8.2   Risk assessment in respect to PPE is the process of determining the capability of the PPE to protect the wearer against a risk which has been identified in the 'general' risk assessment exercise carried out to comply with *regulation 3* of *MHSWR*. In this respect the reason for assessment is not the protection of employees against a given risk, but assessment of the PPE to ensure that it can provide the protection required.

When risks have been identified from *regulation 3* and measures to eliminate or reduce these risks are being considered, it is important to bear in mind that *PPE* is to be regarded as a 'last resort', only to be adopted if the risks identified cannot be controlled by other, more permanent means. If, following the exploration of other ways to eliminate or reduce a risk, it is concluded that *PPE* is the only viable option, it is important that a PPE risk assessment is carried out.

Effectively this means defining the characteristics which the PPE must have in order to combat the risk or risks in question, (taking into consideration any risks which might be posed by the selected

PPE) and comparing the resultant specification with PPE available on the market.

Patently this process must take place before the event, i.e. before persons undertake the work or are exposed to the risks.

In common with all risk assessments, the PPE assessment must be reviewed if there is reason to believe that it is no longer valid, or there has been a significant change in the circumstances for which the PPE is used as protection. Where the re-assessment highlights the need for changes, these must be made.

Control of asbestos

Control of Asbestos at Work Regulations 1987, as amended by the Control of Asbestos at Work (Amendment) Regulations 1998

8.3 The above are the principal regulations in respect to asbestos; other regulations relate to licensing, etc.

Risk assessment in respect to asbestos must be carried out before any work begins, with the objective of identifying the type of asbestos, establishing the nature and degree of exposure which the work will entail, and determining measures to reduce exposure to the lowest level reasonably practicable.

A copy of the risk assessment must be kept at the place or places to which it refers for the duration of the work. See also paragraph 8.4 – Plan of Work.

It is the duty of employers to assess asbestos related risks to their own employees and any other people who may be affected by the work activity. Self-employed people must assess asbestos risks to themselves if working independently. The standard of performance required for assessments is that they are 'adequate'.

Management of work with asbestos, including plan of work

8.4 The principal control and management tool is the 'plan of work', which must be developed before any work to remove asbestos from buildings, structures, etc. takes place.

The plan should give details of the location, nature and expected duration of the work, as well as of the asbestos handling methods, protection and decontamination equipment for those involved, and the protection equipment for any persons who might be affected by the work.

A copy of the plan of work must be kept at the place or places to which the plan refers, and retained there for the duration of the work. It is the responsibility of employers to ensure, so far as is reasonably practicable, that the work is carried out in accordance with the plan.

The plan of work will be one of the measures to reduce risks in terms of the general duty in respect to risk management and control in *regulation 3* of *MHSWR*.

Other control measures include statutory notification of work with asbestos, monitoring, provision of information, instruction and training for employees, provision of respiratory protective equipment (RPE), maintenance and regular examination of local exhaust ventilation (LEV) by a competent person, maintaining strict cleanliness and hygiene standards, clear identification of 'asbestos areas' and 'respirator zones' and provision of medical surveillance and maintenance of health records.

Control standards

8.5   The overriding requirement is that exposure to asbestos should be reduced to the lowest level reasonably practicable.

Without prejudice to the above, there are two specific standards, referred to as 'control limits' and 'action levels'.

Control limits

(a)   For dust consisting of/containing chrysotile:

—   0.3 fibres per millilitre of air averaged over any continuous period of 4 hours;

—   0.9 fibres per millilitre of air averaged over any continuous period of 10 minutes.

(b)   For dust consisting of/containing any other form of asbestos, including mixtures of chrysotile and other asbestos:

—   0.2 fibres per millilitre of air averaged over any continuous period of four hours;

—   0.6 fibres per millilitre of air averaged over any continuous period of 10 minutes.

Action levels

These refer to one of the following cumulative exposures to asbestos over a continuous twelve-week period, namely:

(a)   where exposure is solely to chrysotile (white asbestos), 72 fibre-hours per millilitre of air;

(b) where exposure is to any other form of asbestos including crocidolite (blue asbestos) or amosite (brown asbestos) either alone or in conjunction with chrysotile (white asbestos), 48 fibre-hours per millilitre of air; or

(c) where both types of exposure occur separately during the twelve-week period concerned, a proportionate number of fibre-hours per millilitre of air.

However, where reduction of employee exposure to below both control standards is not reasonably practicable in cost-benefit terms, employees must be provided with suitable and approved respiratory protective equipment (RPE) in order to reduce the concentration of airborne asbestos inhaled by employees to a level below the specified 'control limit'.

Health records and other documentation

8.6   Health records are key to the monitoring of possible ill-health effects from working with asbestos. Where employees have been exposed to asbestos above the 'action level' the employer must keep the health records of those exposed for at least 40 years, and the employees concerned must undergo medical surveillance carried out by Employment Medical Advisers or appointed doctors.

In addition to the special arrangements when potentially hazardous exposure has occurred, pre-employment and periodic medical examinations thereafter must be arranged by employers, who must also provide facilities for the medicals to take place.

All certificates issued by medical practitioners in respect to these examinations must be kept on the employees medical file. In addition to the specific recording requirements in these regulations relating to medical matters, details of all asbestos surveys should be kept for at least five years. Plans of work need only be kept for the duration of the work to which they refer.

Reviewing the assessment

8.7   The asbestos risk assessment should be reviewed regularly, and a new assessment substituted if there is reason to suspect that the original is no longer valid, or there has been a significant change in the matters to which it refers.

Producing the risk assessment

8.8   The 'technical' nature of this subject is such that the advice of the company health and safety adviser/s appointed *vide regulation 6* of

MHSWR should be sought before finalising the risk assessment relating to work with asbestos.

Risk assessment documentation

8.9   The plan of work (see paragraph 8.4) will of necessity contain information specific to the particular job for which the plan has been prepared, but the 'actions to eliminate/reduce risk' column in the risk assessment documentation (see Chapter 6) could include, *inter alia*, the following statement relating to risks from asbestos:

(i)   Pre-work asbestos survey carried out;

(ii)   Plan of work produced (plans available for perusal);

(iii) Use/application of a 'safe system of work' for work involving asbestos;

(iv)   Employee health records maintained (for 40 years).

Notes:

(a)   The plan of work will contain all the specific arrangements for the job in question, including the protection arrangements for people. It is, and should be, job specific.

(b)   The 'safe system of work' in this case can be a generic system complementing the specific plans of work. This can contain the arrangements/requirements for personal protection, cleanliness and hygiene, medical surveillance, delineating areas of risk, reporting concerns, emergency arrangements, asbestos control limits, training and monitoring arrangements and all other key information pertaining to health and safety when carrying out work involving asbestos. This is a 'generic' document.

Both items of documentation (ii) and (iii) should refer to the other. For example a note should preface each plan of work stating that the plan should be read in conjunction with the 'Safe System', while the safe system should be prefaced with a note emphasising that the safe system is *not* a substitute for a plan of work, but a supporting document to it.

Lead

The *Control of Lead at Work Regulations 1998*

Assessment

8.10   The purpose of risk assessment in these regulations is to determine the nature and degree of exposure to lead. Employers must make the assessment in respect of their employees and other people at work on the premises where work with lead is being carried on. Assessment should take place before work with lead commences.

Where the assessment concludes that there is a likelihood of significant exposure to lead, employers have a duty to ensure that a suitable procedure is in place to measure the lead in air concentration.

In these regulations 'significant exposure' means an exposure to lead where:

(a)   employees are, or are liable to be, exposed to a lead in the atmosphere concentration which exceeds half the lead occupational exposure limit (OEL);

(b)   there is a substantial risk of lead being ingested by employees;

(c)   there is a risk of skin contact with lead alkyls or any other substances containing lead which are capable of being absorbed through the skin.

Assessments must be reviewed and revised if there is reason to suspect that they are incorrect, there have been material changes to the work, or if requested to do so by a statutory inspector.

Controls

8.11   Where exposure to lead cannot be prevented it must be adequately controlled by appropriate control measures. The use of *PPE* should only be considered as a last resort, i.e. if adequate control cannot be achieved by other means.

PPE should be suitable and sufficient and compliant with relevant standards. Respiratory Protective Equipment (RPE) may need to be provided in addition to other control measures if exposure to airborne lead cannot be prevented or adequately controlled. In this context, inhalation of lead is deemed to be adequately controlled if the lead occupational exposure limit (OEL) is not exceeded.

Lead – occupational exposure limits (OELs)

8.12   OELs for lead, over an 8 hour time weighted average, are:

—   0.15 mgm 3 concentration of lead (other than lead alkyls) in the atmosphere;

—   0.10 mgm 3 concentration of lead (in lead alkyls) in the atmosphere;

Monitoring

8.13 Following the initial assessment, monitoring must be carried out at intervals no longer than every three months if the exposure to lead arises wholly or partly from lead alkyls; otherwise the interval between each occasion of monitoring may be increased to a maximum of 12 months providing:

— there has been no material change since the last occasion of monitoring;

— the lead in air concentration for each group of employees has not exceeded 0.10 mg/m3 on the two previous consecutive occasions of monitoring.

Records or a suitable summary of them must be kept available for at least five years.

Employee information and training

8.14 Employees must be provided with suitable and sufficient information, instruction and training so that they understand the risks posed by exposure to lead, and the precautions which should be taken. This includes taking care of PPE/RPE, wearing it at all times when prescribed, returning it to its proper store after use and reporting immediately any damage or fault with the equipment.

Other precautions include high standards of personal hygiene, and refraining from smoking, eating or drinking in areas where lead is or could be present.

Increase in exposure to lead

8.15 In the event that a significant unintentional increase in lead exposure occurs, access to the affected are must be restricted to personnel provided with suitable PPE, and whose presence is required to undertake any repairs, modifications, etc.

Care of protective equipment

8.16 Protective equipment must be kept in a clean, efficient condition and in good working order. Local exhaust ventilation systems (LEV) must be examined at least every 14 months. Other control measures, including PPE/RPE (except disposable equipment) should be tested at suitable intervals. Lead contaminated PPE must be kept on the premises, unless removed and transported in closed containers for cleaning by a suitably equipped external laundry.

Maintaining records

8.17 Records, or suitable summaries of them, should be kept in respect of all maintenance, repairs, examinations and tests for a period of five years from the date of last entry in each case.

Medical surveillance

8.18 Employees exposed to lead where the exposure is significant (see paragraphs 8.10 and 8.12), or where in the opinion of the Employment Medical Adviser or appointed doctor, it is necessary, must be included in a medical surveillance programme provided without cost to them.

Medical surveillance should be initiated before work with lead commences, or in any event not later than 14 days thereafter. Subsequent surveillance should be at twelve month intervals, unless the relevant doctor specifies a shorter interval. Relevant doctors may prohibit any employee from working with lead, or impose special conditions upon them doing so.

All such variations must be entered into the employees medical record, and can only be cancelled or altered by the relevant doctor. Employers must comply with any such prohibitions or restrictions.

If the medical surveillance is to be carried out on the employers premises, the employer must ensure that adequate facilities are provided for the purpose, which the relevant doctor may inspect at any time. The doctor may also inspect medical and associated records and the places where work with lead takes place.

Employees must cooperate with medical surveillance arrangements, by attending for examination during work time and providing any relevant information required by the doctor.

Medical records must be kept by the employer and retained for 40 years from the date of the last entry.

Summary

8.19 The purpose in highlighting the key requirements of these regulations is to provide those responsible for risk assessment with pointers to actions which will be necessary in the event that the initial assessment – see paragraph 8.10 – reveals that there is a significant risk of exposure to lead.

In that event, it will be necessary to show what measures are being taken to control the risks highlighted. It is recommended that for this particular risk, these measures should take the following form and be described as follows:

(a) a generic 'safe system of work' – in this case best described as a Standard Operating Procedure (SOP) which includes a description of the arrangements made by the compiling company to address all the matters appearing in this chapter;

(b) records of tests, inspections, examinations, etc. This will include the initial assessment indicating that significant exposure to lead exists or is likely – see paragraph 8.10;

(c) medical records of employees at risk;

(d) method statements relating to each discrete job entailing work with, or exposure to lead. Each such method statement would be prefaced with a note that it should be read in conjunction with the 'Lead' Standard Operating Procedure – see (a) above.

Noise

The *Noise at Work Regulations 1989* (*NAW*)

Action levels

8.20 The *Noise at Work Regulations* specify three 'action levels' as follows:

- first action level – a daily personal noise exposure between 85 and 90 dB (A)

- second action level – a daily personal noise exposure exceeding 90 dB (A)

- third or 'peak' action level – where the peak sound pressure is at or above 200 pascals.

The daily personal noise exposure is the total exposure over the whole working day (taken as eight hours), taking into account the various noise levels in the working environment and how long a person is exposed to them.

The peak action level is likely to be linked with the use of cartridge operated tools, the noise of a gun fired and similar loud noises. This action level is therefore likely to arise in situations where workers are exposed to a small number of loud sound impulses during an otherwise quiet day.

Noise risk assessment

8.21 It is the duty of employers to ensure that a competent person makes a noise level assessment if the noise to which their employees, any self-employed person working for them, or any other person may be exposed as a consequence of their operations, is likely to reach the first action level or above, or the peak action level or above.

The onus of deciding whether a noise survey is necessary devolves upon employers; a reliable indicator of the need is where two persons two metres apart cannot converse without shouting.

A record must be created for every assessment made, which must be kept available until the next assessment is carried out. Therefore the latest noise assessment must always be available for reference and/or inspection. An assessment must be reviewed if there is reason to suspect that it is no longer valid, and/or there has been a significant change to the work processes or situations creating the noise.

Primary duty of employers

8.22 The primary duty of employers in respect to noise is to reduce the risk of hearing damage to their employees to the lowest level reasonably practicable. Therefore when any employee is exposed to noise at the second action level or above, or to the peak action level or above, the noise must be reduced so far as is reasonably practicable, other then by the provision of ear protection.

Ear protection

8.23 Where employees are likely to be exposed to noise above the first action level, but below the second action level (i.e. between 85 and 90 dB (A)) they may request the issue of suitable and sufficient ear protection.

Where exposure to noise is at or above the second action level or to the peak action level or above, employers are required to ensure, so far as is reasonably practicable, that employees are provided with suitable ear protectors, which when worn properly, will provide protection to the extent that they keep the risk of hearing damage to below the second or peak action levels, as the case may be.

When employers provide their employees with information, instruction and training in respect to these regulations (see paragraph 8.27), it is important to ensure that employees understand that where the noise levels are above the first action level, but have not reached the second action level, the onus is upon them to request the provision of ear protectors if they wish to use them.

Employers duties to non-employees

8.24 It is emphasised that the duties of employers to their employees in respect to noise also extend to other persons who could be at risk from noise which their operations generate, for example self-employed persons working for them, visitors, etc.

Ear protection zones

8.25 Where a premises (or part of it) produces noise which could reach or exceed the second action or the peak action levels, those responsible must ensure that there are suitable signs to warn of the danger to hearing and to demarcate the area concerned with signs etc conforming with Paragraph 3.3 of *Part II, Schedule 1* to the *Health and Safety (Safety Signs and Signals) Regulations 1996.* Such signs should incorporate a warning that it is an ear protection zone, and of the need to wear ear protection when in the zone.

Employers must monitor the situation to ensure that none of their employees enters a hearing protection zone unless they are wearing suitable ear protectors.

Maintenance and use of protective equipment

Employers

8.26 Employers must ensure as far as reasonably practicable, that all the equipment provided by them for the protection of the hearing of their employees is fully and properly used, maintained and kept in an efficient state, proper working order and in good repair.

Employees

Employees required to properly use personal ear protectors and any other measures provided by their employer for the protection of their hearing, and to report any perceived defect or shortcoming in these provisions at once.

Information

8.27 Wherever there is a likelihood of employees being exposure to the first action level or above or to the peak action level or above, employers must provide adequate information, instruction and training to include the following:

— the risks to that employees hearing that the exposure could cause;

— the measures which the employee can take to minimise the risk;

— what the employee has to do to obtain personal ear protectors (i.e. the arrangements for issue);

— the employers duties under these regulations.

Duties of manufacturers

8.28 Where an article manufactured for use at work produces noise which could pose a risk to the hearing of those using or close to the article, i.e. where it has the propensity to create noise levels at or above the first action level or the peak action level or above, the manufacturer or supplier must provide adequate information concerning the noise likely to be generated.

'Noise' risk assessment

8.29 Risk assessment insofar as noise is concerned means establishing whether or not the activities/processes of a business create a level of noise that poses risks to the hearing of employees and others. In many cases there will be little doubt about this, in others the answer will not be clear. However, the need for a noise survey or assessment exists in every case where noise levels are high.

Where the levels are above the first action level, or exceed the peak action level, employers have to take some actions to reduce noise, and further assessments will be needed to verify that the measures taken are effective.

If the noise levels seem high, but do not reach the first action level or the peak action level, good management suggests that adopting all reasonably practicable measures to reduce the noise levels is a sensible thing to do. In these circumstances confirmation (from a noise survey) that the levels do not reach the 'action levels' stipulated in the regulations, means that the risk cannot be classified as 'medium' or 'high'.

The measures that are available to employers to reduce noise (other than by the use of ear protectors) include:

— Better soundproofing (attenuation of machinery). Paragraph 8.28 refers to the duty of manufacturers to provide information on the noise created by their products.

— Selection of machinery/equipment which incorporates inherent noise suppression features.

— Creating/erecting sound barriers between noise generating equipment/machinery and workers.

— Preventing machinery not in use to be left 'idling'.

— Job/activity rotation so that workers are not exposed to unacceptable noise throughout the whole of their working shift.

— Isolation of major noise sources from all work stations, or as many of them as possible.

— Operating machinery at slower speeds where possible.

In terms of the documentation of measures to control noise risks, it is recommended that consideration is given to the development of a Standard Operating Procedure (SOP) covering all circumstances where noise appears to have reached, or is likely to reach unacceptable levels.

The following summary of the above notes on noise will assist in the compilation of a 'noise' SOP:

— all workplace noise is to be reduced to the lowest level reasonably practicable;

— a noise assessment is to be carried out by a competent organisation in order to determine the levels of noise or expected level of noise that will arise, if it is believed that the noise levels might exceed the first or peak action levels determined in the *Noise at Work Regulations 1989*;

— in the event the result is that noise levels do not exceed the action levels stipulated in the *Noise at Work Regulations*, all reasonably practicable measures should be taken to reduce noise levels (examples of 'measures' appear above);

— a copy of the noise assessment is to be maintained and only disposed of when a new assessment is made;

— new assessments must be repeated if there is reason to believe that the existing assessment is no longer valid, or if there have been significant changes to the processes, etc; which are the subject of the current noise assessment;

— if the re-assessment indicates a need for different/additional measures for protecting the hearing of employees, these measures must be implemented;

— if noise levels pass the first action level but have not reached the second action level, employees must be issued with suitable ear protectors if they request them;

— noise reduction by means other than providing ear protection is required if noise levels exceeds the second or third action level criteria;

— provide information, instruction and training for employees about noise risk, how to minimise it, how to obtain ear protectors, etc;

— mark ear protection zones with appropriate notices if noise levels exceed second or third action levels;

— maintain and repair ear protectors and ensure they are worm when prescribed;

— maintain in good and efficient working order all other means of reducing noise/providing protection against noise.

Hazardous substances

8.30   The *Control of Substances Hazardous to Health Regulations 1999 (COSHH)*.

The *COSHH* regulations first appeared in 1988, when their introduction created two 'firsts'. They were the first set of regulations enacted since the enactment of our primary health and safety legislation – the *Health and Safety at Work etc. Act 1974*, that were concerned with health as opposed to safety.

Of greater importance in the context of this handbook, they were also the first regulations to call for risk assessment – in this case an assessment of the risks posed to employees as a consequence of their exposure to substances at work which could affect their health.

Although *COSHH* first appeared in 1988 it has been updated continually since then by amending regulations. In 1999 the regulations were re-issued in their entirety, and the new version became law on 24 March 1999.

Meaning of 'substances'

8.31   Substances in these regulations are not confined to proprietary products available commercially, but extend to substances which either arise naturally or as the product of a work process, for example dusts. A substance may be natural or artificial and in a

Table 1 – Classification of hazardous substances, COSHH symbols and their meaning, safety precautions and emergency treatment.

It is important that all persons who work with hazardous substances or who may be exposed to them understand the information in this table, in particular the safety precautions to be observed and emergency treatment in the event of accidental inhalation, ingestion or spillage on the skin or in the eyes.

Meaning	Symbol	Safety Precautions
Toxic/Very Toxic May cause serious health risk or even death if inhaled, ingested or if it penetrates the skin	Toxic	1. Wear suitable protective clothing, gloves and eye/face protection. 2. After contact with skin, wash immediately with plenty of water. 3. In case of contact with eyes, rinse immediately with plenty of water and seek medical advice. 4. In case of accident or if you feel unwell, seek medical advice immediately.
Corrosive May on contact cause burns or destruction of living tissue	Corrosive	1. Wear suitable gloves and eye/face protection. 2. Take all contaminated clothing off immediately. 3. In case of contact with skin, wash immediately with plenty of water. 4. In case of contact with eyes, rinse immediately (for 15 minutes) with plenty of water and seek medical advice.
Harmful May cause limited health risk if inhaled or ingested or of it penetrates the skin	Harmful	1. Do not breath vapour/spray/dust. 2. Avoid contact with skin. 3. Wash thoroughly before you eat, drink or smoke. 4. In case of contact with eyes, rinse immediately with plenty of water and seek medical advice.
Irritant May cause inflammation and irritation on immediate or repeated or prolonged contact with the skin or if inhaled	Irritant	1. In case of contact with eyes, rinse immediately and seek medical advice. 2. In case of contact with skin, wash immediately with plenty of water. 3. Do not breath vapour/spray/dust.

solid, liquid, gaseous or vapour form. Micro-organisms are also included.

Hazard classifications

8.32   Hazard classifications for substances falling within the ambit of the *COSHH Regulations* are Toxic, Very Toxic, Corrosive, Harmful and Irritant.

Table 1 shows these classifications, the precautions to be followed in order to reduce the risk of exposure, and the emergency treatment prescribed in the event of accidental exposure.

Exposure standards

8.33   There are two types:

Maximum Exposure Limits (MELs)

MELs for a substance hazardous to health means the maximum exposure limit for that substance approved by the Health and Safety Commission (HSC) in relation to the specified reference period when calculated by a method approved by the HSC.

Occupational Exposure Standards (OESs)

OESs for a hazardous substance is the standard approved by the HSC for that substance in relation to the specified reference period calculated by a method approved by the HSC.

The schedule of MELs and OESs is published annually by the HSE in publication EH40.

Paragraph 8.35 – employer's duties, describes the minimum measures necessary in the event that either of these two types of standard are breached.

Exemptions from *COSHH*

8.34   Lead and Asbestos are both the subject of their own regulations, and so are exempt from *COSHH*. Also exempt are hazards which arise due to radioactive, explosive or flammable properties of the substance because it is at high or low temperature or pressure.

Other exemptions relate to substances administered in the course of medical treatment, and total inhalable dust which is below ground in a coal mine.

Employers duties under *COSHH*

8.35 Employers are required to assess the substances they purchase for use as well as analysing work processes, the by-product of which might produce substances which are potentially harmful.

The objective of the assessment is to identify risks and enable decisions to be taken on measures necessary to prevent or adequately control these risks.

In addition to their duty to protect employees, employers should, so far as is reasonably practicable, consider the health of persons not in their employment, but who, nonetheless, could be adversely affected by the employers use of hazardous substances. The duty to non-employees does not extend to monitoring, provision of information and training unless the persons concerned are actually on the premises where the work is being carried out.

A self-employed person is bound by these regulations as though he were an employer *and* an employee, except that the requirements for monitoring and health surveillance do not apply.

Employers must carry out a 'suitable and sufficient' assessment of the situation when employees are to work with substances classified as hazardous (see paragraph 8.32) and to review this assessment regularly and whenever circumstances change.

The primary duty of employers is to prevent the exposure of employees to hazardous substances. Only when it is not reasonably practicable to prevent such exposure can other controls be considered. In this respect, the provision of PPE must be regarded as a last resort, to be adopted only when sufficient reduction in exposure cannot be achieved by engineering controls, for example Local Exhaust Ventilation (LEV) or other means. This principle *does not apply* where the danger is from carcinogenic substances or biological agents.

Where substances have an approved Maximum Exposure Limit (MEL) reasonably practicable measures to reduce exposure must be taken, which in any case must reduce exposure to a level below the MEL specified. Where a substance has an Occupational Exposure Standard (OES) it must also be controlled to the standard specified, or, if this cannot be achieved, the employer must identify why, and take appropriate action to bring exposure levels down 'as soon as reasonably practicable'

Carcinogens

8.36 Where the hazard is from a carcinogenic substance and it cannot be substituted, the following hierarchy of controls is required:

- total enclosure of the process, unless this is not reasonably practicable;

- minimising, suppressing and containing the generation of carcinogenic spills, dusts, fumes, leaks and vapour through the use of appropriate plant, processes and work systems;

- minimising the quantities of carcinogens on site and the number of persons likely to be exposed;

- prohibiting eating, drinking, and smoking that may be contaminated by carcinogens;

- providing facilities for personal washing and premises cleaning;

- designation of areas and installations which may be contaminated (including suitable marking);

- safe storage, handling and disposal of carcinogens (including the use of closed and clearly labelled containers).

If there is an escape of carcinogens into the workplace as a consequence of failure of the control measures, all persons who could be affected must be informed immediately and only those persons required to carry out the necessary repairs should be allowed into the area affected. Such persons must be provided with suitable PPE.

Control measures

8.37 Employers and employees each have duties in respect to control measures. Employers must ensure that all control measures are properly executed and that where PPE is prescribed, it is always worn.

Employees must comply with the control measures, in particular the care of, correct storage and wearing of PPE where its use is prescribed.

Employees must also report forthwith the loss of or any damage to the PPE issued to them, or any other circumstances which prevents them from wearing the PPE when its use is prescribed.

Monitoring

8.38 Employers must monitor the exposure of their employees to hazardous substances where this is necessary to ensure that adequate control of exposure is achieved, or where it is otherwise necessary to do so to protect the health of their employees.

8.39 Statutory Requirements — Part 3

Collective records must be kept for five years, individual records for 40 years.

Information, instruction and training

8.39 Employers must provide their employees who may be exposed to hazardous substances with suitable and sufficient information about the risks created by such exposure and the precautions which should be taken. In particular this information must include the results of any workplace exposure monitoring, and if this reveals that a MEL has been exceeded, the employees concerned or their representatives must be informed forthwith.

Employees involved in collective health surveillance programmes (see paragraph 8.40) must be acquainted with the results in a manner which prevents the identification of any individual.

Where employees or others are involved in work in connection with the discharge by an employer of his duties under *COSHH*, for example the development of a COSHH assessment, they must be provided with the necessary instruction, training and information to enable them to carry out the work effectively and safely.

Health surveillance

8.40 The objectives of health surveillance where employees are exposed to hazardous substances in the course of their work are:

— protection of the health of individual employees by early detection of adverse changes which may be attributable to exposure to substances hazardous to health;

— to assist in the evaluation of measures taken to control exposure;

— the collection, maintenance and use of data for the detection and evaluation of hazards to health;

— to assess the immunity of employees in relation to specific work activities involving biological agents.

Where a doctor responsible for the health surveillance programme certifies that it is necessary for an employee who has ceased to work with hazardous substances to continue to be medically monitored, the monitoring must continue until the doctor agrees that it can cease. Where the responsible doctor certifies that an employee may no longer work with hazardous substances, or only do so subject to conditions, employers must ensure compliance.

Employees required to undergo medical surveillance in company time must present themselves at the place and at the time appointed for the surveillance, and must provide such information as is necessary to ensure that the surveillance is beneficial.

Medical records and places where work with hazardous substances takes place may be inspected by the responsible doctor. Medical records must be kept available for 40 years from the date of the last entry.

Where an employer or employee is aggrieved by a decision of the responsible doctor, either may appeal within 28 days to the HSE.

Stages in the process

8.41 Managing the process of compliance with the COSHH regulations can be briefly summarised as follows:

(a) communication to all staff enjoining them to assist with the *COSHH* assessment exercise by disclosing details of any substances which they use, or which they keep in lockers, cupboards, etc;

(b) issuing an edict that no new substance of any kind may be introduced into the company (or company premises) which does not appear either in the company *COSHH* assessment, or an associated list of approved substances which are *not hazardous* without first having been approved by a designated person (e.g. company chemist/safety officer);

(c) making a 100 per cent inventory of *all substances*, whether or not deemed to be hazardous;

(d) obtaining manufacturers data sheets for every substance;

(e) determining which substances are hazardous using Table 1 and initiating a hierarchy of measures to manage the exposure posed by the substances, i.e. elimination, substitution or mitigation of the hazards;

(f) where a residual risk remains, notwithstanding the above measures, providing PPE to those employees who are exposed, such PPE to be suitable for the task and the wearer, and keep records of the issues;

(g) providing all affected employees with appropriate training on *COSHH* (see paragraph 8.39), based on the conclusions of the completed *COSHH* assessment, arranging to keep copies of the substance data sheets where they can a) be referred to easily by those who work with the substances; and b) so that the relevant data sheet can accompany an employee to hospital in the event they accidentally ingest or are overcome by the hazardous substance;

(h)   initiating and monitoring compliance with an appropriate medical surveillance programme.

Notes on above

8.42   The principal regulation calling for risk assessments – *regulation 3* of *MHSWR* – does not require additional work to be done in respect to risk assessments already carried out to comply with other regulations such as *COSHH*, unless these assessments require review and update.

The *COSHH* regulations first appeared in 1988, five years before *regulation 3* of *MHSWR* became law, therefore *COSHH* assessments should already have been in existence when *MHSWR* came into force on 1 January 1993.

As the other regulations which have been covered in this chapter – *Personal Protective Equipment*, *Asbestos*, *Lead* and *Noise*, also call for some form of risk assessment, it follows that the assessments in each case, as well as the *COSHH* assessment, could 'stand alone' and not be expected to be repeated in the 'general' risk assessment in *regulation 3* of *MHSWR*.

For many businesses and organisations, there may be no requirement to consider noise, lead or asbestos as none of these is present or presents problems, or is ever likely to occur, given the nature of the business. Moreover PPE will not be a requirement in most commercial organisations.

Firms that do have to take account of one or more of these elements, and have addressed them by carrying out assessments, are recommended to make a short reference to the fact in the general risk assessment per *regulation 3* (*MHSWR*). This can be done by noting in the column devoted to management or remedial action 'see separate assessment'. An example of such an entry appears in Chapter 6.

Paragraph 8.41 (a) and (b) refers to employees disclosing the existence of substances in their lockers etc. and the requirement not to bring any substances not in the *COSHH* or approved substances list onto company premises or use such a substance on the company's behalf. This is important in that it not only demonstrates effective control over substances – a key responsibility of management – but avoids the possibility of embarrassment which would be caused if an inspector discovered a hazardous substance which did not feature in the company *COSHH* assessment.

COSHH inventories

8.43 Paragraph 8.41(d) refers to an inventory of all substances, whether or not they are deemed hazardous. There are a number of reasons for this:

(i) having a complete inventory of all substances using the form shown in Appendix 1 provides management with information which they ought to have, if only to demonstrate they are 'in control';

(ii) the information in the consolidated inventory often leads to economies. For example, there may be substantial stocks of a substance that has been in store for many years, having been used for a trial or in connection with a manufacturing process which ended long ago. Disposal of the redundant material could be important in avoiding the possibility of contamination or some other mishap, as well as freeing up valuable storage space;

(iii) in larger businesses, the company-wide inventory may reveal use of particular substances in quantities such that central purchasing of the substance could produce cost benefits, and might also highlight opportunities to consolidate by using fewer substances, or variations of them, without compromising standards or quality.

COSHH data sheets

8.44 Substance data sheets are an essential part of the process, and no manufacturer or supplier of a substance can refuse to provide data sheets without being in breach of *section 6* of HSWA. Many manufacturers now keep records of all firms to whom they send data sheets. The purpose of this is to ensure that in the event the constituents/characteristics of the substance in question change, they can send an amended data sheet to the customer.

There is considerable change in the composition of proprietary substances as manufacturers strive to eliminate any hazardous constituents, recognising that this will make their products more marketable, as well as demonstrating in a positive manner their support for the objectives of the *COSHH* regulations.

In terms of splitting the substance inventory into two parts – hazardous and non-hazardous, data sheets will be a key aid.

Assistance with *COSHH* assessment

8.45   In commercial organisations and those which do not use or generate harmful substances, an in-house team can manage COSHH assessment without difficulty.

However, when substances used or generated include those with hazard classifications, particularly if these substances feature on the HSE list of substances having MEL or OES standards, a competent person should be involved in the assessment process and if qualified to do so, to carry out any analysis necessary.

Otherwise, there are a number companies offering analytical services and expertise who are members of The British Institute of Occupational Health (BIOC), Suite 2, Georgian House. Great Northern Road, Derby. Telephone 01332 298087. The BIOH will provide details of member companies in different geographic regions of the UK.

The Construction Industry

The *Construction (Design and Management) Regulations 1994 (CDM)* – introduction and background

8.46   When the *CDM* regulations appeared in 1994, they heralded a completely new approach to construction work by assigning specific duties and responsibilities to the 'key players' (known as 'key dutyholders') normally involved in a construction project, and calling for the production of two essential items of documentation for every project subject to the regulations – a health and safety plan and a health safety file.

CDM applies to all projects where the construction phase is expected to last more than 30 days or where it will involve more than 500 person days of work. Projects falling within these parameters have to be notified to the statutory enforcement authority, one of the requirements of the regulations.

In addition, projects not reaching the above thresholds are still required to comply with *CDM* if more than five people are involved on the construction site at any one time, although the notification requirement is waived. However, even if the work is such that it falls below the 'five persons' threshold, compliance with *CDM* is still necessary if the work involves demolition.

If the construction work is for a domestic householder, *CDM* will not apply provided that the residence in question is not used for business, although all design work, irrespective of the status of the client or the number of workers involved, is subject to compliance with *CDM* – see duties of designers, paragraph 8.54.

Health and safety plans and files

8.47 The *CDM* regulations are not included in this chapter because they call for risk assessments to be carried out using a special format or special documentation as such, rather that risks have to be published within a process that results in the publication of health and safety plans and files. These plans and files require each of the key dutyholders to play a part. The *CDM* Regulations identify the following as being key dutyholders:

— clients or clients agents;

— designers;

— planning supervisors (PS);

— principal contractors (PC);

— contractors.

Scope of this part of the chapter

8.48 It is not the purpose of this handbook to describe the *CDM* regulations in detail, and this section is therefore confined to issues surrounding the creation of health and safety plans and files, in particular the responsibilities of the key dutyholders in respect to these two essential documents.

The health and safety plan

8.49 Health and safety plans must exist, but they do not have to be sent to the statutory enforcement authority. However, in the event things go wrong, or there is a serious accident, they will certainly be key 'evidential' documents, and absence of such plans will expose those responsible to prosecution.

The health and safety plan for a construction project is a two stage document – the 'pre-tender' plan and the 'construction phase' plan.

Pre-tender plan

8.50 The objective of this plan is to highlight all the potential problems, in particular those that might have health and safety repercussions, *before* any work commences on site – hence the term 'pre-tender'. Although the Planning Supervisor is responsible for the development of the 'pre-tender' plan, it can be produced by other competent persons.

Tendering contractors should have access to this plan in order to ensure that their arrangements (and costs) take account of any special or additional protective measures called for in the plan, which should outline the risks envisaged during the course of the project.

Construction phase plan

8.51 When the Principal Contractor is appointed, he will be responsible for converting the 'pre-tender' plan into a 'construction phase' health and safety plan, i.e. by developing/introducing rules for carrying out the construction work safely. These rules are often referred to as 'site rules', whose objective is the elimination of risks during construction.

The designer or designers for the project have key roles in respect to the 'pre-tender' phase, given their clear and unequivocal responsibility to remove or minimise risks to those carrying out the construction work, as well as those who will subsequently have to clean or maintain that which has been built or altered – see paragraph 8.54 (b).

Health and safety file

8.52 The requirement to produce a health and safety file for every project subject to *CDM* will eventually overcome a gap in knowledge that has created problems for those responsible for the maintenance of buildings – especially older buildings.

While the existence of proper records of installed services, maintenance procedures and other similar data is recognised today as key to efficiency and economy, not to mention safety, this has not always been the case. This has resulted in difficulty when planning alterations, tracing wiring circuits, etc.

As there are a considerable number of buildings in use as workplaces today which were erected up to two centuries ago, it is perhaps not surprising that these important records do not exist, especially so if the building was originally a domestic property.

The purpose in requiring a health and safety file is to ensure that eventually every building used as a workplace will have proper records, thus avoiding or reducing the incidence of accidental severence of electricity and other cables, or the inadvertent removal of supporting walls, lintels, etc.

The health and safety file should contain details of the construction methods and materials used, together with information on how to maintain, clean and eventually demolish the building safely.

The process of development of this 'file' should therefore begin with the designer/s, and be carried forward by the PS to the PC and other contractors involved, so that a complete file (accompanied by all the relevant maintenance manuals, etc) can be handed over to the client on completion of the project.

Clients have a duty to make the file available to all those who are called upon to carry out work which could alter the 'status quo' as described in the file.

In many cases, subsequent work will also be subject to the *CDM* regulations, therefore the planning supervisor for the new work will of necessity, have to rely upon the existing health and safety file as the principal source of information.

Summary

8.53 It is clear that health and safety plans and files, notwithstanding their titles, are in effect documents concerned with the identification and elimination of risks associated with the planning, construction and ensuing maintenance, cleaning and eventual demolition of a structure or part of one.

Key dutyholders

8.54 Responsibilities of key dutyholders in respect to health and safety plans and files:

(a)   Client/Clients' Agent

— must ensure that a health and safety plan exists *before* any construction work starts;

— must ensure that any information that the Planning Supervisor ought to be in possession of when compiling the health and safety plan is provided, in particular information relating to any premises at or on which construction work is to be carried out, and which it is reasonable to expect a person in his position to have;

— on receipt of the project file from the PS when the project is completed, making it available to any person who needs to see it, for example others contractors who will be carrying out work in the building.

(b)   Designer/s

— must ensure that any design which he prepares which is to be used for the purposes of construction includes the need to:

  • avoid foreseeable risk to those constructing or subsequently cleaning/maintaining the structure, or any person who might be affected by such work;

  • focus on combating risks at source rather than applying palliative measures to control risks which could have been eliminated by better design;

  • give priority to measures which afford protection to the greatest number of employees in preference to those which protect individuals;
vprovide information about any aspects of the proposed structure (including articles or substances to be used) that could pose a risk to those carrying out construction, maintenance or cleaning work;

  • co-operate with and provide to the planning supervisor all relevant information about the design proposals which the PS will need in order to assess their effectiveness in health and safety terms and to develop the health and safety plan.

(c)   Planning Supervisor

— Has a pivotal role in respect to construction projects, in particular in ensuring compliance with requirements relating to the health and safety plan and files;

— responsible for the production of the 'pre-tender' phase plan before any construction work starts;

— co-operating with designers and satisfying himself that the designers proposals satisfy the requirement to address risks at source, protect groups in preference to individuals and provide all necessary information about the arrangements for construction and the articles and substances to be used;

— co-operating with designers, the principal contractor and other contractors to ensure that information that should be incorporated into the file is being prepared;

— review, add or amend the file as necessary and pass the file to the client on completion of the project.

(d) Principal Contractor (PC)

— Review the pre-tender plan and from it develop a 'construction phase' plan which must be brought to the attention of all those working on the site;

— Assist the PS by assembling information needed for the file;

— Brief all contractors involved in the project on risks to the health and safety of their staff created by the construction work.

(e) Contractors – pass to the PC details of any risks or potential risks created by the work that they will be doing on the site as well as information relevant to the work that should be included in the project file.

Notes on the above

8.55 It is emphasised that the above summary of duties of the key dutyholders relates only to matters pertaining to the health and safety plans and file. Each of the dutyholders has a number of other responsibilities under the *CDM* regulations.

Work Equipment

The *Provision and Use of Work Equipment Regulations 1998 (PUWER)*

Background

8.56 The above regulations replaced an earlier version introduced as part of the range of new legislation which became effective on the first day of the European Single Market – 1 January 1993.

PUWER consolidates into one set of regulations, a number of subject areas formerly covered by regulations exclusive to each of them. Consequently a number of important regulations have been revoked, including the *Power Presses Regulations 1965*, the *Abrasive Wheels Regulations 1970* and the *Woodworking Machines Regulations 1974*.

The new regulations now cover virtually all equipment used at work, for example tools in a tool box, single machines such as circular saws, photocopiers, combine harvesters, hoists, slings, laboratory apparatus, etc.

As with the *CDM* regulations, the risk assessment requirement for *PUWER* does not call for a different method of assessment or recording. The inclusion of *PUWER* in this chapter is a recognition of the fact that these regulations apply to a huge range of equipment whose use is spread across virtually every firm or organisation, however small and whether or not its operations are concerned with complex or technical work.

Actions to eliminate or control work equipment risks

8.57 As *PUWER* is concerned with such a huge and diverse range of work equipment, it is not possible to provide an exhaustive list of control measures applicable to every item. Therefore this chapter focuses on the specific requirements of the regulations in respect to dangerous parts of machinery, and provides guidance on measures to reduce risk during maintenance activity.

Dangerous parts of machinery

8.58 *Regulation 11* of *PUWER* deals with this subject, and it should be noted that the standard of duty in respect to compliance with this regulation is an 'absolute' one.

Effective measures *must* be taken to prevent access to any dangerous part of a machine or machinery or to any rotating stock-bar, or to stop the movement of any dangerous part of machinery or rotating stock-bar before any part of a person enters a danger zone.

The hierarchy of measures that must be followed in order to comply with the above are:

(i)   providing fixed guards enclosing every dangerous part or rotating stock-bar wherever and to the extent practicable; where or to the extent that it is not practicable, then:

(ii)   providing other guards or protective devices where and to the extent that it is practicable to do so, but where and to the extent that it is not, then:

(iii) providing jigs, holders, push-sticks or similar protection devices used in conjunction with the machinery where and to the extent that it is practicable to do so, but where or to the extent that it is not, then:

(iv)   providing information, instruction, training and supervision.

Note:

This is a strict hierarchy of measures, to be followed in strict order. It is important to record conclusions relevant to each stage if it is not possible to comply with solution (i).

Requirements in respect to guards and protection devices

8.59 They must:

(i)   be suitable for the purpose for which provided;

(ii) be of good construction, sound material and adequate strength;

(iii) be maintained in an efficient state, in efficient working order and in good repair;

(iv) not likely to increase the risks to health and safety;

(v)   not be easy to by-pass or disable;

(vi) be sited sufficiently far from the danger zones;

(vii) where is it necessary to observe the operating cycle of the machinery in question, not to unduly restrict the view;

(viii) be made or adapted to permit the replacement of parts or for maintenance operations to be carried out in a manner which restricts access only to those parts being worked on or replaced, and, if possible, without necessitating the dismantling of the guard or protective device.

Notes on above:

8.60 'Danger zone' is any zone in and around machinery in which a person is exposed to risk to health and safety from contact with a dangerous part or a rotating stock-bar.

A 'stock bar' is any part of a stock-bar which projects beyond the head-stock of a lathe.

Protection against specified hazards

8.61 Employers must take steps to prevent the exposure of employees to the following dangers associated with work equipment use, so far as is reasonably practicable, or if not, to adequately control the exposure.

The measures taken must not, so far as is reasonably practicable, be confined to the provision of *PPE* or information, instruction training and supervision; where appropriate the measures adopted should minimise the effects of the hazards as well as reducing the likelihood of occurrence.

Examples of risks with work equipment:

—   articles or substances falling or being ejected from work equipment;

— rupture or disintegration of parts of work equipment;

— work equipment catching fire or overheating;

— the unplanned or premature discharge of anything which is produced, used or stored in the work equipment;

— the unintended or premature explosion of the work equipment or any article or substance produced, used or stored in it.

Some examples of situations covered by the above:

— a loose board or material falling from scaffolds;

— bale falling from a tractor foreloader;

— molten material spilling from a ladle;

— swarf ejection from a machine tool;

— abrasive wheel bursting.

Actions to control risks during maintenance operations:

8.62
• Disconnection of power supply from equipment;

• supporting any part of the equipment which could fall;

• securing mobile equipment which could move;

• removal/isolation of flammable or hazardous substances;

• depressurisation of pressurised equipment.

Adverse environmental/extraneous conditions

— lighting;

— weather related problems;

— other work which may affect the maintenance work;

— activities of people not at work.

Fire – the *Fire Precautions (Workplace) Regulations 1997* (as amended)

8.63 Every workplace is required to include fire precautions and fire emergency procedures within their 'general' risk assessment to comply with *regulation 3* of *MHSWR*.

Fire fighting and fire detection

8.64 In order to ensure that fire risk is minimised, and that all staff know what to do in the event of fire, the regulations specify minimum conditions, which are:

— a workplace must be equipped with appropriate fire fighting equipment, fire detectors and alarms, which, if not automatic, must be easily accessible, simple to use and their whereabouts indicated by signs (note: 'appropriateness' in the context of the above, is a function of the dimensions and use of the workplace, the equipment in it, the physical and chemical properties of the substances likely to be present and the maximum number of people present at any one time);

— taking the above factors into account, adopt measures for fire-fighting, adapted to the nature of the work, size of the business, and also the possible presence of persons who are not employees;

— nominate sufficient persons to implement the fire emergency arrangements made, ensuring that they are provided with suitable equipment for the performance of this task, and are properly trained to carry it out, again taking into account the size of the business, and the specific hazards involved;

— make any contacts necessary with external emergency services, particularly in respect to rescue work and fire-fighting.

Emergency routes and exits

8.65
— Routes to exits and the exits themselves must be kept clear of obstruction at all times.

— In addition the following must be complied with in order to facilitate easy escape in emergency:

(a) emergency routes and exits must lead as directly as possible to safety;

(b) it must be possible for employees to evacuate quickly and safely in an emergency;

(c) emergency routes and exits must be sufficient in number distribution and dimensions to accommodate the numbers of people likely to use them in an emergency;

(d) emergency doors must open in the direction of escape;

(e) sliding or resolving doors must not be used specifically to serve as emergency exits;

(f) emergency doors must not be locked or fastened in such a way as to prevent them being immediately opened by a person in an emergency;

(g)   emergency routes and exits must be indicated by signs conforming with the *Health and Safety (Safety Signs and Signals) Regulations 1996*;

(h)   emergency signs capable of being illuminated must have emergency lighting of sufficient intensity in the event of failure of mains supply.

Maintenance

8.66   Where appropriate, maintenance arrangements must exist in respect of a workplace and any equipment in it scheduled in paragraphs 8.64 and 8.65, to ensure that it is in an efficient state, efficient working order and in good repair.

Quick reference checklist for Chapter 8: Statutory Requirements Part 3

Requirements	Relevant Paragraphs
Personal Protective Equipment (PPE) – the *Personal Protective Equipment at Work Regulations 1992 (PPE)*	
Where the use of PPE is necessary for the protection of employees, do the arrangements and procedures for its use cover the following;	
— developing a specification for the type of PPE required and comparing this to PPE available.	8.2
— keeping the risk assessment which identified the need for PPE under continuous review, and where the *status quo* changes necessitating a re-appraisal of the PPE in use, making the re-appraisal?	8.2
Control of Asbestos – *Control of Asbestos at Work Regulations 1987*, as amended	
Where asbestos is known to exist, or its presence is suspected, have the following protective measures and complementary procedures been established?	
— Risk assessment carried out prior to commencement of work; assessment to include determining the type of asbestos, nature and degree of exposure that will occur and measures to be taken to reduce exposure to the lowest level reasonably practicable; is the risk assessment, which must take into account risks to employees and others who may be affected, kept at the place where the work is to be carried out?	8.3
— Are plans of work always developed for each project, which contain, *inter alia*, details of location of the work, nature and expected duration, asbestos handling methods, protection and decontamination equipment and arrangements for those involved and measures necessary to protect persons who might be affected by the work?	8.4
— Do suitable supervisory arrangements exist to ensure that the work is carried out in compliance with the plan, and is a copy of the plan always available at the work site/s?	8.4
— Are there adequate procedures to ensure the following: notification of the work is made, monitoring, provision of information, instruction, training and RPE, regular examination and maintenance of local exhaust ventilation, maintenance of strict standards of hygiene, identification of 'asbestos areas' and 'respirator zones', provision of medical surveillance and maintenance of health records?	8.4, 8.5, 8.6, 8.7

Lead – the *Control of Lead at Work Regulations 1998*
If work with lead is carried out, do the protective arrangements and procedures include the following:

— assessment of the risk of significant exposure to lead, with arrangements to review the assessment when changes to the *status quo* occur?	8.10
— monitoring to ensure that lead levels do not reach occupational exposure Limits (OELs)?	8.12, 8.13
— provision of information and training for employees	8.14
— dealing with unintentional increases in exposure to lead	8.15
— care of protective equipment	8.16
— maintenance of records	8.17
— medical surveillance	8.18

Noise – *Noise at Work Regulations 1989*

— Is there a procedure to highlight the need for noise assessment, acting upon its findings and retaining an assessment until a new one is carried out?	8.21
— Do all employees concerned know what their rights are in respect to hearing protection, and their duties in regard to using, looking after, storing and reporting loss of or defect in the protection provided to them?	8.23, 8.26
— Have employees been properly briefed/trained in respect to the law on noise protection, the dangers of not complying with the arrangements made to protect their hearing, and other relevant matters?	8.27
— Are ear protection zones clearly identified and the rules made in relation to these zones strictly enforced?	8.25
— Does everyone working in a noisy working environment, including management, understand the meaning of, and statutory requirements relating to the three 'Action levels' defined in the *Noise at Work Regulations 1989*?	8.29

Hazardous Substances – *Control of Substances Hazardous to Health Regulations 1999 (COSHH)*

— Is there a complete inventory of all substances in use, whether the substances are hazardous or not?	8.41(c), 8.43
— Have all employees been properly briefed on the purpose of, and requirements for compliance with the *COSSH* regulations?	8.39, 8.41(g)
— Is the company *COSHH* assessment up to date, and is there a procedure to ensure that it is kept under regular review?	8.41(d), (e), & (f)
— Where hazardous substances are used, is there a hierarchy of control measures to reduce exposure to the lowest level possible, and in any event to comply with the control requirements when substances are subject to MEL or OES standards?	8.33, 8.35

— Where the *COSHH* assessment identifies a need for regular medical surveillance, do adequate procedures exist to ensure compliance with the regulations in this regard?   8.40

— If a carcinogen risk cannot be eliminated by substitution, is the required hierarchy of controls followed?   8.36

Construction – the *Construction (Design & Management) Regulations 1994 (CDM)*

— In the development of health and safety plans for the pre-tender and construction phases, and in respect to the preparation and publication of the health and safety file for the project, is the identification of risk the prime consideration, together with measures to eliminate the risks identified, or to reduce them to the lowest level possible?   8.50, 8.51, 8.52

— Do the key dutyholders as listed below, understand their contributory role in the identification and elimination of risks during the project?

    • client   8.54(a)
    • designer/s   8.54(b)
    • planning supervisor   8.54(c)
    • principal contractor   8.54(d)
    • other contractors   8.54(e)

Work Equipment – the *Provision and Use of Work Equipment Regulations 1998 (PUWER)*

— Do you have a complete inventory of what constitutes 'work equipment' *per PUWER*?   8.56

— Has a risk assessment been carried out to identify risks for each item of work equipment in the inventory?   8.56

— If you use machinery, is protection provided in accordance with the hierarchy of measures set out in PUWER?   8.58, 8.59

— When work equipment is being maintained, do procedures exist to ensure that accidents cannot occur?   8.62

Fire – the *Fire Precautions Act 1971/the Fire Precautions (Workplace) Regulations 1997* (as amended)

— Does your general risk assessment from *regulation 3* of *MHSWR* include assessment of fire related risks?   8.63

— Is special attention given in this aspect of the risk assessment, to areas/workplaces/workstations which are isolated, unusual in any way, or which would be difficult to escape from easily in an emergency?   8.63

— Are you satisfied that the fire emergency arrangements in your organisation meet *all* the criteria set out in the *Fire Precautions (Workplace) Regulations 1997* (as amended)?   8.64, 8.65, 8.66

9 Risk Assessment — The Way Forward

Learning curve

9.1 The effect of the requirement to assess and manage workplace risks has been profound, yet it is fair to state that although this requirement has existed for over six years, we are still on a 'learning curve'. If the number of cases of failure to carry out risk assessments, or of doing so but not meeting the statutory criteria that such assessments are 'suitable and sufficient' is any barometer, many firms and organisations are still at the start of the curve.

Failure is not confined to businesses alone. A survey carried out by the Association of Magisterial Officers (AMO), who examined 300 Magistrates' courts in England and Wales, concluded that the majority of them operate in breach of health and safety law.

It was found that 64 per cent of the courts had not carried out a risk assessment, although at the time of the survey the statutory duty to do so had existed for over six years. Moreover the majority of these courts had no procedures or arrangements to deal with violence, scanning for metal devices including knives and syringes or arrangements for advance identification of those appearing at courts with a known history of violence.

Have we done enough?

9.2 Some firms who have assiduously applied themselves to the development of risk assessments and the ongoing management of the risks identified still feel apprehensive lest it should be considered that they have not done enough to satisfy the statutory requirement. Supposing there is a serious accident caused by a risk not envisaged when the risk assessment was developed or reviewed. Will this precipitate prosecution because the risk assessment is held not be 'suitable and sufficient'?

It would be wrong to predict what would happen if an allegation of failure to carry out a suitable and sufficient risk assessment resulted in prosecution, as only the courts can decide a case on the information laid before it. It is to be hoped, however, that the court would take account of the 'reasonable foreseeability' of the accident precipitating the prosecution, as well as mitigating factors such as the manner in which the defendant organisation had approached its duty towards risk assessment.

Cases heard

9.3 Over time, and as more cases relating to risk assessment come before the courts, judicial interpretation of the meaning and intent of the legislation will help to clarify things, and this may point out the need to review the way risk assessments have been carried out hitherto.

Total understanding of every nuance of law is seldom possible, although understanding increases as cases are heard and judgements given, sometimes following appeal.

Role of Employment Tribunals

9.4 Often the matters causing disputes between employers and their employees, are 'employment' related, and as such do not come before the civil courts, but are heard before a tribunal called an Employment Tribunal – formerly an Industrial Tribunal, from whom appeals are heard by an Employment Appeal Tribunal.

A number of cases heard by criminal and civil courts, as well as Employment Tribunals are described elsewhere in this handbook.

Landmark decisions

9.5 This part of Chapter 9 discusses some cases which help us to understand aspects of the requirements of *regulation 3* of *MHSWR* which perhaps were not perfectly clear, and others which may necessitate a change to the approach currently being taken by some employers to risk assessment.

Pregnant employees and new mothers

9.6 The case of *Day v Pickles Farms Limited* heard before an Employment Appeal Tribunal, is reported in full in Chapter 7, paragraph 7.20.

In essence the judgement in this case means that where an employer employs women of child-bearing age, and whether or not any of these employees are pregnant, are breast feeding or have given birth to a live child within the past six months, the employer must nonetheless consider within the risk assessment process whether any of the work activities or tasks of such employees would be harmful to them, or to their live or unborn children if they were pregnant or new mothers.

In short, this means that a risk assessment should exist for these categories of employee, whether or not there are any at the time the risk assessment is developed.

Thus an employer, once informed by an employee that they are pregnant, can immediately make reference to the 'pregnancy' related risk assessment which has already been prepared, to ensure that the work which the pregnant employee is expected to do does not pose a risk to the employee or her unborn child.

Guidance on the risks to be avoided and the work that employees in the categories described must not do, appear in Chapter 7, paragraphs 7.13–7.14.

Extreme care should be taken when developing special 'pregnancy' risk assessments; it is often the case that while a particular job has almost no elements which could pose a risk to the pregnant employee, however, some elements could affect such an employee – these follow.

Contractors

9.7   Chapter 2, Paragraph 2.11 referred to the necessity for co-operation with others with whom an employer shares a workplace.

In two recent criminal cases, judgements have made plain that when an employer retains the services of contractors to carry out work on his behalf, this does not absolve the client employer from responsibility for the manner in which the work is executed, or for its subsequent failure.

(a) HSE v Port Ramsgate and others

In September 1994, a high-level walkway collapsed, killing six passengers; seven passengers were seriously hurt. Heavy fines were imposed upon Port Ramsgate Ltd although the defective walkway was designed and installed by contractors-engaged by them.

(b) R v Associated Octel Ltd [1994] All ER 1051

In this case a sub-contractors employee was badly burned in an accident while cleaning a tank in the client's (Associated Octel) chemical plant.

In both of these cases charges were brought under *section 3* of *HSWA 1974* which requires employers to conduct their operations in such a way as to avoid exposing persons not in their employment to risks to their health and safety.

Case (a) is particularly interesting in that it is unlikely that the defendants could have had the technical knowledge and skills necessary to recognise any defect in the design for the walkway in question; nonetheless they were found guilty. Thus the accepted wisdom that when an employer engages experts to carry out work which they are not technically qualified to do, it absolves them from criminal liability, has been overturned.

Case (b) resulted in appeal to the House of Lords. In this case the appellant (Associated Octel) did have some involvement in the way that the contractors work was done in that they required contractors to work under a 'Permit to Work' system which was overseen by their own staff. However, the appellant argued that although the contractor was employed to clean tanks on their premises, it was the contractor who had broken the law, because the accident occurred during the course of his (the contractors operations), not theirs.

The House of Lords dismissed the appeal, holding that it was a matter of fact that cleaning a tank in the appellants chemical plant must be considered part of the conduct by them of their operations, albeit that the work itself was carried out by a person not in their employment.

In the judgement, their Lordships stated that each such case of this kind would have to be determined by the particular circumstances. In this instance the work was carried out on the appellants premises, but if an accident occurred in the dry cleaners where the appellants office curtains were being cleaned, or in the garage where their sales manager's car was being serviced, there could be no change against them under *section 3* in normal circumstances.

It will be clear from these two cases that co-operation with others in the process of developing risk assessments is essential, not only when two or more unrelated employers share a premises, but when an employer retains the services of a contractor to carry out work which he does not wish, or is technically not qualified to do.

Of course the problem is that if they are not qualified, employers cannot be fully assured that the method of work proposed by their contractors is safe and without risks to health. Although the employment of competent staff or external consultants to review method statements, systems of work, risk assessments and other relevant documentation provided by contractors will reduce the possibility of failure, it is clear that if the worst does happen, the client employer will have no protection against the possibility of criminal charges, although he may pursue others for breach of contract or in tort.

Duty of HSE to explain risk assessment defects

9.8   In November 1998 a Scottish Criminal Appeal Court held that an accused company is entitled to be told of specific details of alleged deficiencies in its risk assessment.

Although the case itself (i) was not directly concerned with risk assessment per *regulation 3* of *MHSWR*, a previous similar case that did involve *regulation 3* was referred to as a precedent.

The circumstances were that a company gave instructions to a person not in their employment to carry out a task which caused him to be severely injured; they were prosecuted under *section 3(1)* of *HSWA* for failing to conduct their undertaking to ensure, so far as is reasonably practicable, that persons not in their employment were not exposed to risks to their health and safety.

The specific offence was in not carrying out an adequate and sufficient risk assessment to determine what the risks associated with the operations were, in order to develop a safe system of work to ensure that the task was carried out safely and without risks to health.

In the first court, the Sheriff decided that the charge under *section 3(1)* of *HSWA* was specific enough, and that the defendant company should stand trial. The company appealed to the High Court of Justiciary.

The prosecutor had argued that the event of the accident itself was enough on which to base the case of an inadequate risk assessment; however, the appeal court did not accept this proposition.

A previous case considered was *Carmichael v Marks & Spencer plc [1996] SLT 1167*.

In the Marks & Spencer case – which was brought for a breach of the risk assessment duty per *regulation 3* of *MHSWR*, the appeal court found that there was the same requirement to give details of alleged inadequacies in the *MHSWR* risk assessment as are applicable to cases brought under *HSWA*.

This argument was reinforced by the fact that there must have been a detailed investigation after the accident and before charges were brought, which would have provided the prosecutor with enough information to make detailed charges.

The court therefore allowed the company's appeal.

(i) 1999 SLT 492

This means that in the event the HSE or local authority Environ-mental Health Officer where appropriate, take action in the event they consider a risk assessment does not satisfy the requirement that it is 'suitable and sufficient', they must detail the specific defects in the Enforcement Order or notice of prosecution.

Prosecutions under other legislation/regulations

9.9 In May 1998 the Dean and Chapter of Westminster Abbey were prosecuted under *section 2 (1)* of *HSWA 1974* following an acci-dent in which an employee had fallen between joists in the abbey roof, sustaining multiple fractures; they were fined £5,000.

The stipendiary magistrate commented that the Abbey had failed in its supervision and must take on board that employee's might disregard employer's instructions.

In this case a risk assessment had been carried out which con-cluded that the risk of falling was low. The injured employee had not been given a specific method statement on the precautions required when carrying out the work.

A number of prosecutions for offences, particularly those brought under *sections 2* and *3* of *HSWA* (duties of employers to their employees and to persons not in their employment respectively) arise due to the absence of a risk assessment, or, although an assessment exists, it is deemed not to effectively address the risks identified by the assessment.

In these cases, there may be charges brought under *sections 2* and *3* of HSWA and *regulation 3* of *MHSWR*, or, as in this case, the charges are confined to the *HSWA* offences, although it is clear from the evidence that the risk assessment per *regulation 3* of *MHSWR* was considered not to be 'suitable and sufficient'.

Millennium bug

9.10 Although there is no specific legislation relating to the potential problems arising from the inability of some computers and com-puter systems to recognise and act upon dates after 1999, there is widespread recognition of the problem, which is referred to as 'date discontinuity'. Accordingly the government have set up a working group to provide advice and assistance to business and industry. This working group is titled 'Action 2000'.

Every organisation and business (as well as individual households) must assess the potential for disruption and possibly danger, arising from this problem.

In terms of business and industry, the effect – if things do go wrong – might be confined to commercial/administrative disruption. However, across a very wide spectrum of industries and occupations, failure of systems can have serious, sometimes catastrophic consequences. Examples are the transport industry (airline operations in particular), hospitals, traffic signals on roads, systems that control the maintenance of buildings and many others.

Whilst it is important for everyone – businesses, organisations and individuals to ensure that their computer systems are able to cope with the millenium problem, or if not, are being modified to do so, the HSE have made clear that where they have enforcement responsibility, they will prosecute firms or organisations who, through their failure to properly address this matter have placed their employees or others at risk.

The Millennium problem clearly represents a risk to every business and organisation, albeit to different degrees, ergo this risk must be considered within the general risk assessment arrangements.

Given the topicality of the subject and the fact that HSE Inspectors and local government environmental health officers (where appropriate) are focusing on the Millennium problem in their work programme, it is important to ensure that this risk appears on every risk assessment, irrespective of the risk classification assigned it by those carrying out the assessment.

In Chapter 6 paragraph 6.2 emphasis was placed on the advantages in recording every risk which has been considered by the company, irrespective of its category or ranking.

This advice is most apposite in respect to the Millennium problem, given its topicality, and the fact that visiting inspectors will require to see tangible evidence that the problem is being properly addressed.

Millennium problem – advice and guidance

9.11 The Government's working group 'Action 2000' have published a number of guidance booklets, of which 'Health and safety and the year 2000 problem' is among the most useful.

Other relevant publications include:

— Safety and the year 2000 – A research report containing methodology for prioritising and rectifying safety related systems. HSE Books 1998 ISBN 0 7176 1491 3 – £15.

— Embedded systems – a guide to evaluating how this problem could affect your business – Free from Action 2000. Tel: 0845 601 2000.

— Managing year 2000 conformity: a code of practice for small and medium enterprises. Disc PD2000–2, BSI 1997 ISBN 0 580 27445 4 – £14.95 British Standards Institution, 389 Chiswick High Road, London W4 4AL. Tel: 0181 996 9000.

— INDG283 Contingency planning for a safe 2000.

— INDG287 Year 2000 risk assessments – both the above free from HSE Books.

The risks associated with the Millennium are, or should be transitory, and in that sense they are unique. However, the potential for serious and/or lasting problems affecting so many organisations makes this risk the most important and all-embracing since the introduction of *regulation 3* in 1993.

Risk assessment here to stay

9.12 Although universal compliance with the requirements for risk assessment as set out in *regulation 3* of *MHSWR* has not been achieved, the level of acceptance and degree of conscientious participation is now at a high level.

On the minus side there are those who regard development of a risk assessment as a chore – necessary but an irritation.

Frequently their motivation to produce risk assessments is not recognition that these play a key role in the health and safety equation, but a request to provide a copy to a client whose health and safety arrangements include the requirement to see the assessments of all the firms that they do business with, or at least those who provide services or carry out work on their premises.

In many cases confirmation of the superficial manner in which the assessment has been carried out appears in the assessment documentation itself. Risks are identified with a single word – 'falling' 'electricity' 'collision' are examples – while mitigating measures are couched in similar shorthand, for example 'training' 'experience' and 'procedure'. Where assessments in this format are published, it is difficult to imagine how those reviewing the document can feel comfortable that it meets the 'suitable and sufficient' criteria.

In Chapter 1 the importance of risk assessment becoming part of an organisation's 'culture' was discussed. Experience shows that while those directly concerned with the development and ongoing review of risk assessments remain focused and committed, the remainder of the workforce, even if they were involved during the initial exercise to develop an assessment, no longer retain an interest, probably considering that their initial involvement was enough. This inertia can only be countered by ensuring that the risk assessment message and objectives are highlighted at every opportunity. Company publications, house journals, department meetings and notice-board announcements are all useful vehicles for keeping the risk assessment message in the forefront.

Whenever any change is contemplated, such as workplace design, moving departments, new equipment, new processes, shutting-down operations and the myriad other changes that occur in business and industry, the effect upon the risk profile must be a prime consideration. Moving departments around, often following changed design or rebuild of the accommodation, is often completed before anyone notices that the fire exit and exit directional signs are no longer correct; sometimes they are dangerously misleading as a result, thus placing all those relocated at risk. Yet this risk must have manifested itself when the move was planned, and if appropriate action had been taken at the planning stage, the correct emergency signing could have been in place on day one.

Real success in achieving a 'risk related' culture will have been reached when the need for such elementary risk combating measures is recognised at the beginning, not after the event, and not only by those responsible for move planning, but by every member of staff.

Measures to keep the momentum going

9.13 Chapter 2, paragraph 2.6 discussed the requirements of *section 2(3)* of *HSWA* – Health and Safety Policy and *regulation 4* of *MHSWR* – Health and Safety arrangements.

It will be evident from reading this paragraph that the arrangements for and frequency of review of the risk assessment must be published in the Health and Safety Policy and/or the arrangements called for by *regulation 4* of *MHSWR*. Failure to do so, given the pivotal role of risk assessments in the overall equation, is unacceptable and would attract criticism if not action by the HSE or local authority, as appropriate.

However, once the arrangements are published in either or both of the documents referred to, they must be followed. If the frequency of review is stated, and it should be, then it will be an easy matter to verify that the review has taken place, and there can be no acceptable excuse for not carrying out the review.

Many organisations use their own internal audit departments to verify that reviews – and indeed any other actions whose periodicity is stipulated in company procedures, have been carried out – and on time. This useful internal verification resource should not be overlooked.

Conclusion

9.14 The overriding principle concerning workplace health and safety is that everyone at work has a part to play. However well intentioned, no measure to protect workers from harm can succeed without their co-operation, and measure to protect workers will not be effective without the commitment of management.

Within the overall health and safety umbrella, risk assessment is no different to these principles. Managers should never presume to decide what the workplace risks are without consultation with those that take the risks, and those who do take the risks owe it to themselves, their colleagues and to their employers to make a positive contribution to the risk debate.

9.14   Risk Assessment — The Way Forward

Quick reference checklist for Chapter 9:
Risk Assessment – The Way Ahead

Requirements	Relevant Paragraphs
— Do you have a model risk assessment prepared addressing work tasks which could be harmful if carried out by employees who are a) pregnant, b) have given birth to a live child within the past six months or c) who are breast-feeding, even if there are no employees in these categories at present? NB: This does not apply to employers who do not employ women of child-bearing age.	9.6
— Have you considered, in discussion with your health and safety adviser, the implications of the *R v Associated Octel* case for your business if it uses the services of contractors?	9.7
— Are you satisfied, and can you demonstrate that the measures taken in your business to ensure that no 'Millennium 2000' exposure exists, are either completed satisfactorily, or are progressing as planned? Is there a suitable entry in this regard in your risk assessment?	9.10, 9.11
— Given the importance of risk assessment, are you satisfied that communication on this subject is meaningful and motivating?	9.13

Index

Index

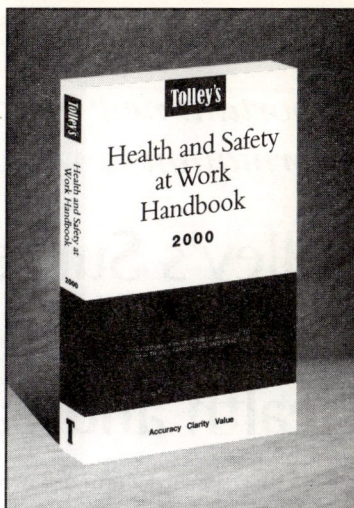

Tolley's Survey of Senior Executives' Committment to Health and Safety 1999-2000

The level of commitment provided to health and safety managers by board directors and senior executives is a key issue identified by RoSPA. **Tolley** has therefore commissioned this management report so that health and safety managers can compare and evaluate their working practices against other peer organisations and assess the level of commitment from the board on health and safety matters.

The full report of this topical survey among both senior executives and safety managers is based on data extracted from quantitative questionnaires circulated to **Tolley's Health and Safety at Work** magazine and **National Health and Safety Group** members. The report discusses the following key performance indicators in this area:

● Safety cultures
● Safety committees
● Training of line managers in safety
● Communication and dissemination of information
● Health & Safety responsibilities
● Support from board of directors on safety
● Performance measurement and monitoring

Tolley's Survey of Senior Executives' Commitment to Health and Safety 1999-2000 has been prepared with meticulous detail to provide you with useful and practical information.

Product Code: SSEC00   ISBN: 0 7545 0496 4   Price: £49.95   November 1999

Money-back Guarantee

You can order **Tolley's Survey of Senior Executives' Commitment to Health and Safety 1999-2000** on 21 days approval. If you choose not to keep it, simply return it to us in a saleable condition within 21 days and we will refund your money or cancel your invoice, upon request.

How To Order

Tolley's Survey of Senior Executives' Commitment to Health and Safety 1999-2000 is available by writing to: Butterworths Tolley, FREEPOST SEA 4177, Croydon, Surrey CR9 5ZX
Alternatively please call our customer services team on: 020 8662 2000 / Fax: 020 8662 2012

Butterworths   **Tolley**

A member of the Reed Elsevier plc group

25 Victoria Street, London SW1H 0EX
VAT number: 730 8595 20
Registered Office Number: 2746621